Miigwetch
Nancy - for being a
friend and editing grandfather
book - you're a treasure to have

Grandfather's Blood Memories and Unbroken Spirit

Sharon

Frank Doolittle
Gigawaabamin

This storytelling is dedicated in memory of a grandfather I never knew.

Grandfather's Blood Memories and Unbroken Spirit

As Told by Sharon Doolittle Shuck
Granddaughter of Frank Doolittle

Grandfather's Blood Memories and Unbroken Spirit

ISBN 978-0-9890478-4-5

Printed and bound in the United States of America

Publication assistance and book layout and design by
Marlene Wisuri, Dovetailed Press LLC

Dovetailed Press LLC

ARROWHEAD REGIONAL ARTS COUNCIL

This activity is made possible in part by the voters of Minnesota through a grant from the Arrowhead Regional Arts Council, thanks to appropriations from the McKnight Foundation and the Minnesota State Legislature's general and arts and cultural heritage funds.

CLEAN WATER LAND & LEGACY AMENDMENT

Tarpaper Shack Press

tarpapershack39@gmail.com

We are the chosen. In each family, there is one who seems called to find the ancestors.

To put flesh on their bones and make them live again, to tell the family story and to feel that somehow they know and approve.

Doing genealogy is not a cold gathering of facts, but instead, breathing life into all who have gone before. We are the storytellers of the tribe.

-Unknown

Table of Contents

Introduction

I was born in 1939 on "the Rez," the backwoods of Brookston on the Fond du Lac Reservation. There were five of us kids and two parents living in a tar-paper shack.

Early on, stories were told, Elders spoke in Ojibwe, about smudging of healing plants, the Eagle feather, fishing, gathering and hunting in the traditional ways. My grandparents protected, taught, and kept the grandchildren safe from boarding schools. They kept the families together.

As I reached adulthood, I furthered my education and became a nurse. I heard from my family about my dad's father, sentenced to Leavenworth prison. I wanted to learn more. I had the writer's itch.

I lacked the confidence to be a writer. So I enrolled in writing classes and also joined two writers' groups. They gave me encouragement and support to publish my grandfather's book.

I never imagined I would be publishing a book at this late stage of my life. Many Natives and non-natives have heard about my grandfather, Frank Doolittle, his boarding schools, and Leavenworth Prison. They wanted to hear more. Fond du Lac Historical Society, writers' groups, and Adult Learning Center instructors encouraged me to write and publish his story. Many said, "His story needs to be told."

For many years, I heard rumors and storytelling about Frank Doolittle, my father's dad, from my brother Fred, but it was not until my sister obtained records and a mug shot from Leavenworth Prison that I began to learn the full story. Instructors, researchers, and elders navigated technology and found documents, photos, and boarding school records.

Because I am telling my grandfather's story through his voice in the first person, I write in the "Rez accent," the broken English he learned at boarding schools. Grandfather did not learn the basic 3R's. Carlisle boarding school placed him in level 4; he was 18 at the time. Using his voice is essential in telling the story.

I feel it is very important for me to tell his story, while I am still able, so that history is not forgotten. The historical images and documentation I have gathered as an elder, support the blood memories I heard through storytelling of cultural genocide, forcing Native children to learn English and assimilate into the white culture. My grandfather was one of those Native children at Indian boarding schools.

I want his story passed on to the younger generation of Native and non-Native people, who we are and where we came from, to understand the region's history and historical trauma that our ancestors went through.

- Sharon Doolittle

Chapter 1

Arrivin' at the Ashland train depot in northern Wisconsin, I make ready to leave the passenger car, 4 days fadin' into the past since boardin' my last train ride from Kansas City, Kansas. On this day, July of 1918, The *Halfway Through the Summer Moon*, I am Frank Doolittle, inmate 11707, a free man, born durin' the *Flower Moon*, May of 1886. Limpin' along down the aisle of the train to the metal steps, weak from hunger, unsteady, one foot steps down. From behind, a heavy foot pushin' me forward, fallin' flat on my face, the train's wood platform. A hand from out of nowhere, touchin' my painful shoulder. Turnin', lookin' up at him, *eya*', one of my people, an *Anishinaabe*. Noddin' to each other, his eyes movin' to my shirt collar, he nods again. His hand reachin', touchin' Leavenworth prison number 11707 sewn into my shirt collar. His eyes knows where I come from. He reaches out liftin' me upright, holdin' tight on my right arm. Grippin' pain, shootin' up and down my arm, I do not give way and show my brother my weakness. Noddin' to him, I speak, "Where headed my brother?"

He speaks of his brother, jailed in Madison, steppin' over the border of the reservation at the Bad River Reservation at Sanborn. Noddin', *eya*', another federal crime.

Starin' at his Medicine Bag tied to his breeches belt with twine, my hand reachin' up, touchin' the fine glass beads sewn into the soft buckskin. Wonderin' to myself, what healin' medicine does my brother have inside his medicine bag? Sage, tobacco, sweet grass, maybe cedar? Will he share his medicine with me?

Readin' my thoughts, his hand reachin' into his bag, handin' me a pinch of *asemaa, manoomin*, and dried fish. *Eya'* for my journey home.

Thinkin' to myself, the Spirits are with you, my brother. Lookin' into the bag, an Eagle feather. He dares not use it. *Eya'*, another Indin offense. *Eya'*, The Great White Father in Washington writes many federal crime laws to prosecute Indins. *Eya'* remeberin', buyin' whiskey and Leavenworth.

Noddin' to my brother and walkin' away from me takin' notice, shoulder slumpin' forward, head down, whisperin' to myself, *Eya' Miigwech* my brother, *Gigawaabamin.* Feelin' burnin' eyes on me, the railroad ticket agent pointin' to a rough wooden sign that reads: "No Indians Allowed." *Eya'*, anothcr offense.

Castin' my eyes down, the hot wooden platform burnin' the soles of my feet, a toe sticks out from well-worn prison boots. Hobblin' along away from the sneerin' eyes of the white settlers, I notice a half-breed Tribal Police eyein' me. Strugglin' with each step, stabbin' pain up and down my legs. My empty belly feelin' like it will leave me. My right arm bleedin'. The half-breed, sneerin', grinnin', tobacco drippin' from his mouth, his club slappin' against the palm of his hand, waitin' for me to make the wrong move. Lookin' at him, smellin' his snuff, I wish for a good chew. Leavenworth did this to me.

Thinkin' back sixteen moons ago, I was once strong, sturdy, wise like my father, Chief James Doolittle, feedin' my people, an apple orchard on tribal allotment land, huntin', gatherin', fishin' feed my people.

Now, a skeleton of a man, wastin' away with white man's disease, flesh hangin' from my bones, I'm old before my time. Inchin' along slowly, with every step, Leavenworth shackles now taken off have left their lastin' marks on my ankles and wrist now swollen and blacken with old blood.

Hissin', clankin', screechin' of wheels, the train steam whistles startles me. Breakin' into a cold sweat and fallin' again on the platform, I gather myself on all fours, makin' my way to an open clearin', a whiff of sweet grass enters my lungs. There I will rest until my clan people arrive with the team of horses with buck wagon.

Feelin' squeamish, dizzy, the belly swellin' in want of food, throat parched from thirst. My thoughts slippin' back to that last train ride, watchin' old men passengers chewin' snuff, spittin' into a rain barrel fill with warm green water, they cough up gray foamy spit, wippin' it on their fine woolen coats. Most likely, my thoughts, the old men have the white man's cough. Consumption, the white plague. That green smelly water, I could not drink. *Eya'*, but soon I will reach the shore line of the great water and have a cool, clear drink of Mother Earth's sweet water.

Halfway through the *Summer Moon*, the sun reachin' its highest place, beatin' down on my tired, old body of thirty two years. Chewin' on my brother's dried fish gift, the belly still wants for more. *Eya'*, rememberin' back, so many moons ago when I was mighty strong, it's berry pickin' time, eatin' red sweet berries, juice drippin' from my mouth, fillin' my belly, drinkin' swamp tea, having a good chew.

Hearin' Grandfather, Chief *Kish-ke-ta-wug* spirit words through the winds, he speaks of the Great White Father in Washington, passin' laws against the Indians. No liquor, no *pow-wow*, no feastin', no funerals and no settin' foot outside the reservations. Lips quiverin', sorrow fillin' my heart, my clan people will not be here! I am too weak to walk! How will I get to the long house? Will I journey on to the other side? *Eya'*, a tree, a good place to rest and think.

A quick glance I have an eye on a large oak tree, waitin' to shade me, a good place to rest. Catchin' a whiff of newly mowed hay, the smell of bark, sweet grass and berries, the seasons comes to mind, *Great Spirit Moon*—storytellin' time; *Sucker Moon; Maple Sugar Moon*; the *Flower Moon*—when the Creator put me on Mother Earth; *Ricin' Moon*; the clans feasts, gathers and powwows. My people will do this again. Closin' my eyes, a sense of fear overtakes me. Will I pass to the Spirit word under this tree I rest under? There is much daylight to think. Father's, the Chief, words comes to mind, "Son, it is better to listen, think before you speak your words." *Eya'*, this is what I will do.

Restin' my head against the old oak tree, eyes drowsy, ready for short nap and in the distance, hearin' the sounds of wheels, whistle blowin', a train is leavin' the Ashland Depot. Thankin' the Creator, I'm not on that train.
Eya', a free man.

Chapter 2

This oak tree I lean against, only if I had this throughout my life. But here in Ashland, I have an aged one to lean on. What has this tree witnessed? How many children has it seen get on trains to be taken away? Blood memories spillin', rememberin' back to my childhood, at Carlisle, Odanah, Flandreau Indin Boardin' Schools, are cloggin' my brain.

The long house, thinkin' of the long house, Elders, my people, my clan people, makin' ready for a feast, a celebration, a piece of fry bread, *manoomin*, the smell of sweet grass, cookin' fish over the camp fire, drinkin' clean water, eatin' sweet red berries, and havin' a good chew.

Pickin' up last night's thoughts as though I never drop them, wishin' for the smudgin' of cedar, tobacco, sage, and sweet grass, a cool dip of sweet water to heal me of Leavenworth Prison. Coughin', hunchin' over, pain overtakin' me, breakin' into a cold sweat. Back at the prison, a white army doctor barks, "Who has T.B. in your family?" I tell him. "My mother, she has T.B." Did I bring this T.B. to their prison?

Driftin' off, my people, will they come for me? Will we talk? Will we *pow wow*? Will we Feast? Will Elders gather healin' plants? Will they mend my broken body? Will they speak their Ojibwe? Will they walk quiet in their soft deer hide moccasins and fetch me? Will the half-breed Tribal Indin be eyein' through the thick brush? The fear of that rips my belly apart.

Grandfather spirit words comes to me, "My son, you must not hate, help our people, the government takes our land. Remember this." "*Eya*', Grandfather, this I will remember. Today Grandfather, I am a free man, without irons, to gather, hunt, and fish. I will thank Mother Earth, Creator, smoke a pipe in the Four Directions.
This is what I will do."

Stillness in the air. I hear a movement in the brush, maybe a deer. Listenin', chirpin' birds, insects, woodpeckers knockin' tree trunks, calmness overtakin' my body. My thoughts slippin' back to the fourth and last train ride, my last time at Leavenworth, my survival, a long sentence, a crime for buyin' 10 pints of whiskey at a Bad River white saloon. The prison fed me sour food, bugs crawlin' in mush, and water down tea. The guard and his club, beatin', shacklin', keepin' me in a dark dungeon he calls, "a Indian cell." Now this July 1918, I am free, free to walk in sunlight, free to return to my people, my village, free to drink Mother Earth's clean clear water. Free at last.

Thinkin' of that guard, that guard and his club, shackling' me, walkin' from behind, groanin', gruntin' with every step. "Warden Morgan orders Frank Doolittle to his office." I am told, by the prison guard, "the warden has papers for you to see." Flinchin' at those words, I become weak, clammy with sweat. A letter! Another letter from Louise?

Takin' by surprise from Warden Morgan, he hands me prison release papers. I am to leave Leavenworth. I served my time. An early release for "Good Behavior." A one way train ticket to Ashland, Wisconsin, three days ration, $3.28, a grip, a blanket, and clothin'. The guard will see me safely home! Noddin' my head yes, lookin' down at my feet, cringin' at his words, sour mush comes up to my throat.

The guard and his club! He will see me home! The guard who beats me with his club! The guard who stands behind me, slappin' his bully club into his hands, keepin' the drunkin' Indin in line for good behavior. Gettin' even because I am Indin! Feelin' the club touchin' the back of my neck, sweatin' with fear, thinkin', will I survive the three days with the guard? Pointin' his club to the open door, it leads to an open court yard.

Lookin' up, the warmth of the bright sun is welcomin'. A shadow shades my vision. Sensin' his presence, *Migizi* sweepin' closer, circlin' above me, openin' his wide wings, swoopin' down and droppin' his gift at my feet. My bony hands, now hangin' with flesh, pickin' up *Migizi* feather, noddin', I say "*Miigwech.*" My stiff crooked fingers gently touch the soft gift, nuzzlin' it against my lips. Hearin' faint sounds of flappin', swishin' of wings, gazin' up to him, noddin'. He circles above, waitin', he will protect and guide me on the long journey home. Back to Bad River, to my people.

A driver, a paddy wagon, and guards wait. I am a free man. I do not need a paddy wagon! Leavenworth, warden, and guards think I will run! Run to where? They are after my $7,000.00 allotment money! They think I am a rich Indin! Leavenworth jailers, they line their pockets, chargin' me for dental, food, and medical bandages!

Grandfather's Spirit Ojibwe words come to me,
"Remember son, where you came from, this land is our home, our blood. It is inside you no matter where you go."
Grandfather, he says, has seen the tribe change since the 1854 Broken Treaty. He tells of sadness, the danger of whiskey, and the way his people were being treated.
"Yes, Grandfather, I understand your words."

Chapter 3

The guard, his club, we board the train in Kansas City, Kansas. The club points to two tattered leather window seats, away from the eyes of fellow passengers. My clothin' I wear, an old torn prison stripe garb, with stitchin' sewn into the Leavenworth coat collar, inmate number 11701. Passengers in fine wool clothing, starin', sneerin', and spittin' on me. It is best that I look down and remain silent.

Peerin' out dusty crack window, strainin' my eyes, countin' rails, buildins', cars, the train jerks, rollin' slowly away from the city. *Eya'*, this is good. July's boilin' sun, a scorchin' day. A gentle breeze will come when the train picks up speed. It will be good to get away from this wasteland of Kansas.

Lookin'out, listenin' to wheels changin' tracks, swayin' back and forth, countin' whistles at each crossin', last the prison guard's gruntin', snorin' his heavy breathin' puts me at ease. I'll get some quick shut-eye, holdin' tight to my grip in my lap, closin' my eyes to the trains rockin' movements. Driftin' off, thinkin', I am a free man.

A cough awakens me. My cough! Lookin' out shatter window, where the sun meets Mother Earth low in the western horizon, seein' rays of light filterin' between tall stacks of field corn, an image of me, returnin', I am a farmer again, plantin' three sisters: corn, squash, and beans on tribal allotment land. Grandfather, the Chief passes down his tribal land to Father, the Chief James Doolittle. When Father journey on, it was pass on to me.

Mother Earth will provide food for my people, plantin' puttin' down tobacco *Miigwech* to the Creator. My clan people bellies will be full to the gills. They will not hunger in pain again.

Break into a cold sweat, recallin' a memory I cannot forget. The *Great Spirit Moon*, January 18, the year of 1918. Icy stiff fingers press on cement wall. Frost! Smellin' human waste comin' from the slop pail. The guard has not empty it in days, full of clumps of ice pee. My bony hands cannot break a hole, I think, where do I relieve myself?

Wearin' a thin stripe prison garb, my number 11701 sewn into a shirt pocket. I cover myself with the small pox blanket, the wool gives me some warmth. Stiff crooked fingers pokin' through holes, rats eatin' my small pox blanket! For sure, the rats will get the white man's disease, T.B.

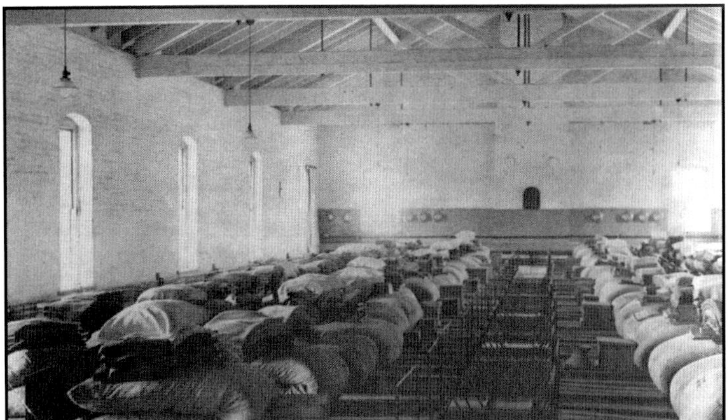

Prisoner Dormitory at United States Penitentiary
Leavenworth, Kansas

Chapter 4

Hearin' heavy footsteps, kneelin' and puttin' my ears to the floor, *eya'* it is him, draggin' the club against the iron bars. Listenin', the steps come closer. The sound sendin' cold shivers down my spine, the sound, echoin', bouncin' off the walls.

Raisin' to my feet, movin' close to a wall, away from the iron bars, seein' him walk pass the cell, I take a deep breath, a sigh of relief. His footsteps stop. He turns, backtrackin' to the cell, sneerin' at me, tobacco juice drippin' from his yellow teeth. The fat belly hangin' over his belt. His red face looks like a pork hog, gaspin' for a breath. His neck is larger than his puffy face. Wet with sweat, hands reachin' forward grabbin' the iron bars, most likely to steady himself. Sittin' back, I wait for him to speak. Gruntin', clearin' his throat, he tells me, "'The warden sends for you! Another letter from your wife, Louisa Starr! Shackles on!"
My wife! Louisa Starr!

The Warden sends for me! The guard tells me of a letter from Bad River. A letter! A letter from Bad River! Louisa's letter! Louisa wrote to me in prison! Her family, the Starr's, what have they done while I am in prison? My land! My allotment land! Louisa cannot read or write English words!

Takin' no kindness, the guard, yankin', rubbin' the cold irons tight against open wounds, wrist and ankles oozin' with blood, pushin' me into the catwalk, chains are heavy, cuttin' and openin' up more flesh.

Walkin' in silence through long cold damp dark tunnels, every step an effort, the chains feel like 10 pounds on each leg. Hearin' his heavy breathin' from behind, I'd best be careful with that guard and keep one eye open. Will the club make a strike from behind? Will I live through this distance of time to the warden headquarters?

Warden Morgan hands over a letter dated January 7, 1918, from the Stearns Company Store on the Bad River Reservation. The letter reads, "The Stearns has charged to your account for provisions for the Starr family." I tell the warden I will not pay for any supplies that were not purchased by myself, and decline to sign the check to pay Stearns.

Who wrote that letter for her? I know that white Indin agent, Sam Campbell. He's in cahoots with the crooked sawmills, the Stearns Sawmill Company. Sam is cheatin' the Natives and linin' his pockets with my money!

Louisa never went to Indin boardin' school. Once, she told me, before we had an Indin Ceremony in November of 1914, she was born in the village of Sawyer on the Fond du Lac Reservation. She was five at the time when the government agents came into the village and kidnapped children, takin' them to Indin boarding schools. Her family hid Louisa in the backwoods of Sawyer. The Catholic priest and nuns never found her.

The Treaty of 1854, the treaty my Grandfather signed, Chief *Kish-ke-ta-wug*. It was he who said, "The white government in Washington D.C. signed an agreement, gave the Bad River 120,000 acres of land in the village of Odanah." Another white treaty is broken. Now it is 1918, my reservation, my people have lost more than half of our land, given to the white settlers and sawmill company.

Louisa and her family are signin' their X's on my allotment land papers and buyin' supplies at the Stearns Company Store in my name! They take me for a damn fool. A fool I was to marry her and take in her family. I gave the Starr family shelter for three long years. I will get behind their trickster ways. I will visit the Stearns Company Store and the Allotment Office when I get on my feet again. This is what I will do!

Father, James Doolittle, Chief *Wegimawebitang*, with his passin' in 1913, his allotment land was passed on to me.

Hearin' Grandfather Spirit, heavy with sorrow, he speaks Ojibwe, "I was the signer of the 1854 Treaty, believin' the treaty would allow my people to live in peace, but the agreements were soon broken. My son, do not sign the white government papers and give the land to white settlers, or the government, fight for our land. This land was given from the Creator, we must protect Mother Earth. I am told, and it is written, I have much land, the hillside slopes of Bayfield shoreline where the sweet red apples grow. The Bureau of Interior governments show my land value is $7,000.00."

Yes, Grandfather, I will listen to your wise words. The government will not take my land. I will fight for the land. I will sign papers over to my two sons, Joseph and *Gwi wi sens* (Little Boy/Frederick) Doolittle.

Group portrait of Ojibwe Chiefs from Bad River, Lac Courte Oreilles, and Lac du Flambeau, in Washington, D.C. Chief *Kish-ke-ta-wug*, seated on chair, second from left.

Chapter 5

Thrown in jail in Madison, waitin' a transfer to Leavenworth Penitentiary—word comes to me, my two boys, Joseph and *Gwi we sens* were taken by the Indin agent's nun to a Catholic Indin boardin' school in Hayward Wisconsin.

Fred, *Gwi we sens,* the youngest, I hear is an altar boy. Like me, he stealin' the priest wine and Joseph, big and clumsy for his age, milks cow in the barn, spillin' milk. Nuns beatin' him with sticks. I hear he does not cry out.

Mary Houle, my first wife, went back to her people on the Fond du Lac Reservation in Minnesota. Feelin' her pain, our boys, Joseph and *Gwi we sens*, our hands cannot reach and touch them, heal or hear their silent cries.
The Catholic priests, nuns, Indin agents, why does their white God torture his chosen children?

Prayin' to *Gizhe-manidoo*, the Creator "Help my boys. Do not let them suffer shame, pain, or beatin' like I had at the Sister School in Odanah, Flandreau School in South Dakota, and Carlisle Indian Industrial Boarding School in Pennsylvania.

On the second day of freedom, night fall begins. The train wheels keep me awake. I'm a bit hungry but decide to save the rations for tomorrow. Drowsy with sleep, I'm a free man, a free man at last. I'm rid of Leavenworth.

Awakenin' to shriekin' wheels, peerin' out the broken window, stench of rottin' cattle smells, the train is stoppin' in a stockyard. The guard speaks, "We're in Chicago stock yard." I remain silent.

Reachin' down for the grip, my hands are feelin' the floor. Fear, sick to my belly, a bad feelin' overcomes me. My grip is gone! Lookin' at the prison guard he turns his head away from me. I say nothin'. Tremblin', my grip, $3.28, and three days rations gone! Thinkin' to myself, the guard stole my grip, he is a thief! I cannot accuse him! He will club and send me back to Leavenworth!

I am two days without rations. The train conductor does not offer Inmate 11701 any fresh water or food. Watchin' the guard, he eats my rations and not offerin' me a bite. The club lies across his fat belly. Hurtin' from the hunger, pain, and thirst I close my eyes. Dozin' off again, my clan people will feed and fill my belly with Mother Earth food.

Restin' my head against the passenger window, hearin' train wheels clankin', squeakin' on the rails, countin' the whistles blowing at each crossin'. Eyes heavy, yawnin', fightin' off sleep, watchin' the guard.

Chapter 6

Another vision appearin', we brothers and sisters, the village *Mindimooyenh*, countin' on her fingers, she speaks Ojibwe, our children are 60 moons, 5 years old in 1891, when the Black Robes came into our village and seized them from our mother's arms. I cry for mother. Black Robes, grabbin', pushin' children onto the waitin' wagons. Grandmothers wailin', "Where are you takin' our children?" *Mindimooyenh* says, "Little boys do not cry." But still I cry. Starin' back at Mother, Father, sobbin', tears flowin' down my brown face, I see Mother, she too is cryin'. Why are we cryin'? Mother's hands trying to grab and touch me. Reachin' and stretchin' my skinny arms toward her, I cannot reach her hands. Cryin' words again, "Our children, where are they goin'?"
The Black Robes do not answer.

The Black Robes, standin' by teams of horses, wagons, backlit by the sun, hooded caps shoulder to shoulder, holdin' long sticks, mouth curled up, their piercin' eyes burnin' into my flesh. *Maaji-manidoo*, a bad spirit came into our village. A stick swings back and forth and hits my face. Seein' white stars, then black. Hurts shootin' up my cheek and deafens my ears.

I awake to cryin'. It is me cryin'! I cry out in Ojibwe, "Help us! We do not want to go!" Our people's hands tremblin', faces wet with tears, mothers fallin' to the ground. I am afraid. Who will feed me? Who will take care of me? Who will speak Storytellin'? Buryin' my face into my hands, I cry.

Mindimooyag, they say, "Little boys do not cry."

Walkin' into the sunlight towards the waitin' wagons, mothers runnin' to the children, they say, "Do not forget our ways." My eyes blurry with tears, I will never forget my people. I cry for my mother. I cry for my father. Black Robes, grabbin' my hair, pullin', and draggin' me across the wet grass to the wagons. Mother's outstretch arms tryin' to touch me keenin', "Do not take our children!" I cannot reach her! The Black Robes do not speak to mothers.

My people drawin' closer together, weepin', watchin', tryin' to pull children back. Father, the chief is touchin' me, the Indin agent's club hittin' his arms, the sound of crackin' like a tree branch is broken. Black again.

Father, Chief James Doolittle, a strong, wise leader, gatherin' his people, he speaks, "Our children will be taken from us. This is the white man's law! The priest and nuns will teach our children the white man's ways. They will learn English, schoolin' and be baptized Catholic. That is the way. The white man's way. There is nothin' I can do to save our children. I have spoken."
I was five at the time, and did not understand his words.

Daylight comes to the Sister School in Odanah. Awakenin' to whimperin' of brothers and sisters, we're in a large room, with a straw mat and a small pox blanket. Reachin' to a brother, touchin' his hand, we whisper in Ojibwe, "Is this the Catholic Indin School?"

Speakin' with our hands, duckin' from the Black Robes, the storytellin' we hear from our Elders, they say, Indin children are taken from the villages, send off to Catholic schools, many miles from their reservation, to learn the English ways, plow fields, go to mass, and serve the priests. Some children never come home to their people.

Slippin' back to a vision, I'm a child of 60 moons at Odanah Indin School. Lookin' again, it is nightfall, sleepin'on a straw mat, coverin' myself with a small pox blanket, a sound awakens me, swishin' back and forth. Is it a big rat, draggin' its tail across the wood floor? Peerin' out from under the blanket, seein' dark shadows movin' in the darken room. Somethin' is being dragged! Tremblin' with fear, the shadows driftin' to the foot of the straw mat, coverin'myself and hidin' under the small pox blanket, I pray in Ojibwe, "Father, Father, come for me. I do not like this place!"

The image stays, hearin' many cries, noise, loud draggin', dark shadows hoverin' over my bed, shiverin' with fear, soilin' my small pox blanket.

Mornin' comes, east light creepin' into the large dark room. I am wet, cold, and afraid. Why am I cold? My eyes followin' the sun rays, stoppin' on bare straw mats and no small pox blanket. Where are my brother and sisters? Did the dark shadows take them into the night? Never to be seen again? It is halfway through the *Summer Moon*, berry pickin' time. The white nun speaks of July. What is July? I do not understand her white words.

Mother Earth gave her people the woodlands, to gather, to fish and to hunt. But at the Sister School, my belly swellin' with pain, my skin loose and hangin' on bones, long arms and legs did not fill out. At night while sleepin', my dirty fingers reach out and scratch open sores, cuts and bruises. The Indin agent spoke of me as not much of a book learner, dumb, lazy, not strong. He puts me in the field to plow, every day, day after day, mornin' till the sun falls behind the earth. More pus and blisters came through the skin from plowing the fields, the harvest to feed the priest, nuns, and Indin agents. At dawn every day, after the Catholic mass, harness to leather straps, a mule pullin' me across the open fields, plowin', weedin', and seedin'. Little time was spent in the classroom, learnin' to read, write, and add the English ways. Priest, nuns, they say, Frank Doolittle, a lazy Indin, a good farmhand.

The vision continues. Sneakin' away from the wood school buildin' at night, my eyes watchin' for dark shadows to follow me, keepin' low, crawlin' along the wet grass, like a green snake. Tall corn fields ahead, a good place to hide. I hear my people gatherin', weepin', drummin', and burnin' a fire.

Rememberin' when I was baptized a Catholic at the Sister School in Odanah, the white priest pickin' me to be his altar boy, to serve him, givin' me sips of wine and bread. Soon, I learn to steal and drink the wine to forget the shame, sorrow, and loneliness. Priest, nuns, and Indin agent kept beatin', yellin'and starvin' we brother and sisters. "Indian children are evil. Now you are the children of God."

Leave *Changin' Color Moon* at the Catholic sister school in Odanah boardin' school. Soon, I will be of age, fifteen, too old for mission school. I will be free of the government Indin mission school. I keep stealin', drinkin' the priest's wine, shuttin' my eyes tight and forget unwanted touches, neglect, and abuse. The priest words, you are uncivilized and need to be saved from your wicked ways. The priest he speaks, "You are child of God."
But I do not like his white God!

I once ran away from Sister School, the Indin agents caught me walkin' in the fields. They brought me back and tied me to a tree. They tried to kill the Indin out of me, beatin'me with sticks. Father, the Chief, heard of the beatin', he sends word, "Do not cry out, my son, do not let the Black Robes know how you suffer."

A half-breed Indin agent orderin' all students to the front of the Sister School Little Church. I am smilin' on my last day of school. The agent will tell me to go home to my people. Lookin' up at the church steeple, an iron bell, I will miss the ringin' of the beautiful bell sound, ringin' all over Odanah.

Indin boys at school learn to fight, we all wanted to ring the church bell, swingin' from the bells rope so it could be heard all over Odanah. Soon we brothers were stealin' food, blankets, and fightin'. Some students were caught, beaten and put in the stockade for days. I learn to fight with my fist. Father, the Chief, hearin' of this, he spoke, "My son, Indin boys do not fight with brothers and sisters. This is wrong. The Creator is angry with your fightin'.

But at the Sister School, it is a place where bein' Indin is wrong."

Thinkin', I ask, "Why does the White God let the priest and nuns beat my brothers and sisters? This I do not understand." The Chief did not answer.

Chapter 7

Lookin' to the shorelines, smellin' and seein' smoke risin' above the tree lines, hearin' faint sounds of *mindimooyenh's* chantin' with the drums, givin' thanks for a good harvest. I could run fast to them and hide like a green snake, sneakin' to the canoes helpin' to parch the Creator's gift, *manoomin*.

Crawlin' into the corn fields, my heart is heavy with sorrow, weepin', afraid. I wonder, will I too disappear into the night at Odanah and never be seen again? Never see my people? My head turnin', fear comes within me. Glancin' up, Sister School comes into view. A short crawl through tall corn fields, seein' dark clouds loomin' near, as if almost touchin' me, fillin' my shaken body, a vision, a bad spirit hangin' over the school and church.

My body stiffens. Hearin' rustlin' of corn stocks, movement, a heavy foot is pushin' into my back. A club comes crashin' into my shoulders. I do not cry out. The half-breed tribal police beatin' me with his club.

Mid week, *Wild Rice Moon*, August 1905, we brothers and sisters, wearin' black wool Sunday mass uniforms and high top leather shoes, sweatin' under the heat of the sun, the Indin agent tell us to gather in front of the church. The white nun wants one last picture, her God's children at the Sister School in Odanah, Wisconsin. Sweat drip into my burnin' eyes, then rememberin' *mindimooyenh's* words, "Little boys do not cry." But I am 15, almost a man and I still cry.

The white priest speaks, Catholic Indin students leavin' Odanah, board the train in Ashland and travel by rail west to Flandreau Indin Boardin' School thousands of miles from Bad River, there will be no run-a-ways.

A cold chill overtakin' me, frightenin' and shakin', a sour taste comes in my belly, swallowin' hard, thinkin' to myself, I am fifteen, too old for Flandreau. The priest reads my name, Sister School nuns forcin' me to leave Odanah, they do not want me to see my Father, the Chief again. Was I not a good student, plowin' the fields every day? Milkin' their cows so the white nuns and priest could eat and drink? I went to their white Catholic mass! They beat me and I did not fight back!

Rememberin' *mindoyne* Storytellin', they say, "Children from Flandreau do not return home to their people, some disappearin' into the night, they forget their ways." I pray to the Chief, "Father, father, hear my words through the winds, do not let the white people take me to Flandreau." Will Flandreau Indin Boardin' School feed me stinky, sour, watery soup? Will the school have a fence in the field with sharp wires stickin' out? Will they beat me for sneakin' a bite of potatoes?

A team of horses, buck wagons are hitched up and waitin' at the fence post in front of the church. That day, the Sister School church bell did not ring. There are no brother and sisters fightin' to ring the bell. Lookin' beyond the plowed fields for the last time, the Chief and his people, walkin' to the church holdin' sacks of harvest.

My father, James Doolittle hands me a sack of harvest
for my journey to another Indin boardin' school in
Flandreau, South Dakota.

Father speakin' in a soft tone, "The white government in
Washington has spoken. It is their law. I cannot stop them.
My son, you are the tallest, like a pine tree, long in the arms
and legs, growin' like a spindlin' plant. It is weak at the
roots, not strong. The north wind will blow you over.
Be brave my son. Show no anger. Remember son, where
you came from. Who you are! Who your people are!
Do not forget. Count rivers. Fields. Bridges. Government
states. Towns. Villages. Count days and nights.

You will hear Indin children from many nations. More
than you can count. They will speak their Mother Tongue.
Speak with your hands. This they will understand. This I
know. I have spoken."

Noddin' to father, turnin' my head from the chief, I shield
my waterin' eyes, rememberin', little boys do not cry.
I am fifteen and still I cry in 1903.

Flandreau Indian School, Flandreau, South Dakota

Chapter 8

Another memory returnin', hauntin' thoughts of Carlisle in 1905.

A train car travelin' east to a military old army post in Pennsylvania. A place where the sun greets Mother Earth, crowded with many Nations, Indin children, Dakota, Apache, Cheyenne, Arapaho and Ojibwe. My brother and sisters, Ojibwe Michigan youths speakin' their Mother tongue, their words soundin' strange to me. We speak broken English. I learned to speak the broken tongue from The Sister School in Odanah and Flandreau Indin Schools. Nuns beatin' me if I spoke my mother tongue— Ojibwe. We brother and sisters, arrivin' in the dark of night, dirty, hungry and weary. Pale faces pressin' against the train window to see wild Indins. Town people, waitin' at the railroad station tellin' the Indins to walk up the hill to the Old Carlisle Barracks.

Rememberin' that night, no food, water, clothin', or beddin'. There are no straw mats or small pox blankets to cover with. We Ojibwe did not understand our many brothers and sisters tongues. Soon, we start wailin' into the night. White Indin Agents draggin' out Indin children by their hair. The next daylight, my eyes searchin' for my brothers, they disappear into the night in the old army barracks. Fearin' the worst, I never will see brothers again.
Will I disappear into the night?

At the St. Patrick's Catholic Church in Carlisle, I am the tall one, 6'4", the priest picks me to be altar boy. I began stealin' wine from the cellar, drinkin,' warmin' my cold bruised body. The priest sometimes givin' me sips of his wine, he speaks of helpin' me. Does the wine help me to forget shame of unwanted touchin', beatin', spoil army food and empty belly? The priest and nuns at St. Patrick's Catholic Church they say, "You are the children of God. You will be saved." Who is their Catholic God? Why does their God not save me?

We Ojibwe brothers, separatin' in the corn field, plowin' the fields at the edge of the barracks, a little east of the workshops, an Ojibwe brother, speaks with his eyes, noddin' with his chin, hidden danger in the tall corn field. Hitch to the mule, alone between the corn stalks, a chill covers my body.

Carlisle has a cemetery! A children cemetery! Burial mounds! Fresh dirt! A small grave! A burial of an infant! My heart weepin' for my lost brothers and sisters. My eyes fillin' with water. *Mindimooyenh's* spirit words to me, little boys do not cry. Durin' the dark of night in the old barracks, hearin' whisperin' stories, Carlisle many nations disappear into the night. They disappear to Carlisle cemetery.

A form from behind blackens the dirt, the shadow moves forward, pushin' forcin' my face into the ground between the tall rows of corn stacks. The warmin' of the afternoon sun awakens me, crawlin' to my knees, shootin' pain sends me sprawlin' back to the ground, dark shades of gloom overcoming; me. I will speak to no one. I will remain silent. Rubbin' the eyes of dirt, a feeling of lightness, *eya'*, ancestral spirits have come to me. They speak through the winds, "Chief James' son, the bad spirits are surrounding you, run from this evil place, run to your people, run to your village." *Eya'*, this is what I will do.

General Pratt, headmaster at Carlisle Military Industrial School, speaks of Indin students unfit, lazy to book learn, and will plow fields.

School master, Indin agents, overseer, speaks of me, the tallest, strong, long legs and arms, a slow learner and places me at level 4. I am to plow the fields.

At Odanah and Flandreau, I plow fields, at Carlisle plowin' the fields again, harness in leather, a mule pullin' me forward, tillin' the dirt under, seedin' the soil, gatherin' a harvest and harvestin' crops to feed the white people, the captain, the officers, the school master, the teachers, the guards, and the white Indin agents.

The Eastern sun takin' no pity on me, endless days in the fields, sweatin', fallin', open sores and drawin' blood, a mules pullin' on the neck yoke, bendin' my head forward, openin' and tearin' more flesh.

At the Old Carlisle Barracks, dark into the night, I hear in broken tongues, whisperin', nations speak of seein', a white spirit risin' from the mounds, reachin' upward, cryin', chantin' in different tongues. They say, eyes and ears are playin' tricks, a thick fog, a white owl squealin'. Listenin' to their words, wonderin', maybe our brothers and sisters are callin' to us.

Hearin' Father, the Chief, storytellin', speakin', "Our children are pure, holy, movin' energy. Elders need children to pass their storytellin' to the next generation. I will tell him of the white spirits cryin', chantin', reachin' from the burial mounds at Carlisle cemetery. This I will remember.

This white man's God, this white Catholic God of St. Patrick's Church in Carlisle, the priest, the nuns, they say, "Our God, he will protect his children." Then where is this God? Priest and nuns they say, "All Indians have evil thoughts, have wicked ways and need to be saved by beatin' the spirits out of them." Why does their God let the priest and nuns touch us in their God's House of Prayer?

Darin' not to shift my body, my eyes rapidly circlin', watchin' dark corners, *eya'*, black robes, hidin' near tall pillars. A cloud of back dust hangin' over them. We Ojibwe brother and sisters, we whisper, "*Maaji-manidoo!*" His bad spirit is in God's House of Prayer. St. Patricks' Catholic Church in Carlisle. Evil is near!

An Ojibwe brother, whisperin' our Mother tongue, he hears, priests doin' things behind the church altar. I pray to the Creator. Let their White God send me home.

A brother hands touchin' me, chins motionin' up. Hearin' noise, keys janglin', clickin' of shoes, scrapin' on the hard tile floor. The noise comes closer. Feelin' fear, my body shivers and sweats. The white nun walkin' pass pews, turnin', stoppin' to the pew in front of me. Reachin', the nun pullin', hittin' a a brother across his back, draggin' him from the kneeler. From the corner of my eye, he's lookin' at me, panic in his black eyes. His eyes cry "help me."
He remains silent.

Our Elders, they say, "Do not cry out. Do not look the white people in the eyes. Look away. This is our way." Turnin', I look away from my brother. I do not see my brother again. Hearin' *mindimooyenh's* spirit words, "Children disappear into the night at Carlisle."

Nuns have long sticks, hittin' backs of heads, knees and faces if we speak or fallin' behind in the military walkin' to St. Patrick's Catholic Church for Christian religion. Harsh punishment comes to Indin students who speak their Mother tongue and do not practice spiritual practices.
We students attended masses together, some were baptized, some made their first Holy Communion, a white band on arms of small children, the nuns they say, it means, the innocent of children hearts. Fix in my heart, rememberin' the priest, unwanted touchin' behind the church altar. The Bishop confirms a large number of Indin Catholic students at Carlisle St. Patrick's Church, The *Leaves changing Color Moon*, September of 1905.

Carlisle Indian Industrial School, Carlisle, Pennsylvania

Chapter 9

The next day, plowin' the fields, we brothers lookin' toward the clouds. He's here. Circlin'. *Migizi* his wings spread wide, sweepin' closer. He knows. Our Creator knows. His children hearts are fillin' with sorrow. Noddin' to my brother, I sense a loss, will never see my brother again? Will he not return to his people, to his village? My eyes see a fresh mound of dirt. Did the Carlisle guards take another brother to the Carlisle cemetery?

My heart achin' with pain, eyes heavy, cloudy, fillin' with tears. I am eighteen, and still I cry. Elders Spirits, who passin' through, grieve for their lost children at Carlisle. I do not understand Carlisle "white man" punishments.

A feelin' comes over me, walkin' across the wet grass to my brothers and sisters they rest under mounds of burial dirt, without a name, they never got to go home. Never reachin' the burial mounds, a club from behind strikin' me in the back. I did not cry out in pain, another blow comes. Curlin' long arms and legs into a ball, layin' in the wet dirt, I'm shiverin' in the hot September sun, The *Leaves Turning Color Moon*. Fear fillin' my body. Lookin' from the corner of my eye, the white Indin agent, comes into view, the snitch who rarely strays to the open plow fields, standin', lookin' down at me. White stars fill my head.

Turnin', crankin' my head, rubbin' dirt from the eyes, seein' the sun rays filterin' through the tall corn stocks, my head

swells from pain. Rustlin' of leaves! He is near!
I will talk to no one of this! I will remain silent. Hearin' *mindimooenh's* storytellin' of Carlisle, they say, many children do not return to their families, to their reservations and to their people. Our children, lost at Carlisle.
I will be a run-a-way.

Harnessin' leather straps across my shoulders, a mule pullin' me from behind, plowin' the fields, Ojibwe brothers, they scatterin' seeds. Stoppin', lookin' at my brother, noddin'.

My brother he knows! He sees my eyes! I will run from Carlisle and disappear into the night. Run-a-way! Run-a-way to my people! To my village! This is what I will do. The Carlisle will not make room for me at the burial mounds. I will not speak to no one of this run-a-way.

I plan in the dark of night in the Old Carlisle Barracks, The *Falling Leaves Moons*, dark in October, sneakin' to root cellar, stealin' army food, a sharp knife, a bed roll, hop a box car and head northwest across the corn fields, to my people. My reservation. I count moons, when the leaves turn, I will run.

Every evening after Indin students finish barn chores, Indin agents count Indin heads, pokin' straw mats, checkin' for bodies, the lockin' the barracks thick heavy wooden doors. No Indian student will pass through those doors. No Indin students will run away from Carlisle Indian Industrial Boarding School.

I hear stories. Lakota, three Plains brothers, came to Carlisle two years ago, all were dead, buried in dirt mounds near the plow fields. I hear more stories, beatin', hunger, Indin girls have babies, and sickness from the white man's diseases.

In the dark of night, hearin' an early mornin' train whistle far in the distance to the Old Carlisle Barracks. The Creator hearin' of my get a-way, makin' *Fallin' Leaves Moon* go away behind the clouds. Climbin', passin' through a broken window, crawlin along the wet grass to the root cellar, I'm grabbin' three sister harvest, squash, beans, corn, a small pox blanket, a sharp knife, and throw them into army gunny sacks.

Out in the open field, behind the barracks, dartin', shimmerin' like a snake, I made my way pass the cemetery, wonderin', are there more mounds. I hear stories in the dark of night, whisperin' in Ojibwe, they say, next to the athletic grand stand field, it had its back to the cemetery, more burial mounds, some say, maybe two hundred or more. I think to myself, I will not disappear into the night and have Carlisle cemetery claim me.

I crawl between old buildin', hidin' behind the workshops, a thicket of brush, not far from the railroad track, waitin' for my escape to arrive. Pitch darkness, October 23, 1905, *The Fallin' Leaves Moon* is hidden behind dark clouds. I make no sound, quiet as a hunter, my eyes watchin', waitin'.

Soon, hearin' whistle blowin', clangin' of wheels changin' tracks, smellin' of burnin' coal, kerosene lantern light up the passenger train windows. From where I hide, seein' many nations, cryin' into the night. Brothers and sisters, dirty, hungry, tired. Dressed in traditional buckskin clothin', long black hair, and speakin' only their Mother tongue.

Another brother I hear, plannin', run-a-way from Carlisle, disappearin' into the night, makin' his way to his Plains people in South Dakota. I hear stories of Lakota's people, ridin' horses at Little Big Horn, losin' much buffalo, many people buried, land taken by the Great White Father in Washington.

Thinkin' to myself, I hear stories, Grandfather, the Chief, a signer of the 1854 Treaty, he speaks, "My people do not trust the government. We have lost much land to the Great White Father in Washington."

Keepin' low to the ground, makin' my way to railroad tracks, jumpin' rails, hoistin' myself up into a box car, feelin' wood planks, a strange feelin' comes over me, hearin' voices, broken English! Did the snitch follow me? Will I disappear into the night! Disappear to the cemetery? I keep silent, listen. I do not want the Indin agents to hear me. I do not want to be shackled and thrown into Old Carlisle stockade!

Carlisle stockade! We Ojibwe students, we say, hear stories. Apache boy, 60 moons, nothin' but skin and bones, not marchin' the General Pratt military way, white Indin agent guards beat, drag the boy to Carlisle stockade.
School officials found him three day later. Indin students, they say, Apache boy buried in Carlisle cemetery. He will never return his people or his village.

I listen to hear a voice. Another brother! A run-a-way! Makin his way to the train's box car. I do not cry out.
I think to myself, my brother, he will never return to his Plains people, to his camp, to his reservation, to hunt, to ride, to smoke a pipe. Was the white Indin agent waitin', watchin' for run-a-ways?

Keenin' Native children cries echoin' from inside the box car. My thoughts returnin,' to two moons ago, wailin' into the night, thousands of miles from my village, eighteen and soilin' myself. Big boys do not cry, but still, I cry.

Chief James, my father, I hear him speakin' through the four winds, "Remember my son, count rails, lakes, rivers. Keep eyes wide, ears open. The Creator will keep you safe. I have spoken." Sorrow fills a heavy heart, thinkin' back, will I ever see my people again? Now in the dark of night, I am a run-a-way from this Carlisle Indin School. Father, I remember your wise words. I have counted lakes, rivers, and rails. Creator, I pray to you keep me safe from harm.

I will be a farmer again. But I am only eighteen! I have no plow! I have no money! I have no horse, seeds or land! I have no money! It has been many years since the black robes came to our village and took the Indin children to Indin boardin' schools. Will my people know me?

Native students working in a potato field at Carlisle Indian Industrial School, Carlisle, Pennsylvania.

Chapter 10

Thoughts driftin' back to me, 1917, as if were yesterday. I'm thirty-one years old, prison shackles on ankles and wrists, waitin' to board the passenger train in Madison Wisconsin to Leavenworth Prison Kansas.

A Federal Marshal and a half-breed Indin agent, long barrel rifles slung over their shoulders, clubs in hand, standin' beside me. A wood sign at the ticket agent reads: "No Indians Allowed." Takin' in a deep breath, smellin' sweet clover, thinkin' to myself, how many moons will pass before I will smudge Mother Earth healin' plants, sage, tobacco, cedar, sweet grass. How many moons will pass before seein' my people, my village, my Bad River Reservation, the Long House?

Takin' notice of white passengers dress in their fine Sunday clothin', they walk near me, gawkin', snarlin', spittin' on me. There is much mean Indin talk, "And don't sit next to that drunken Indian!"

Sloughin' shoulders forward, castin' my head down, I do not eye them. Rememberin' Father's wise words, "Do not look the white man in the eyes. Look away."

The Federal Marshall gestures, pointin' his club to the waitin' train. My fourth train ride. I am told a three day travel from Madison to Leavenworth, three days ration, clean water and a good chew.

On that day, no clan family gatherin' around me. No one cryin' for me. A federal agent, I am told, Indins will not leave the reservation. That is the law! I am alone, tied to irons, alone with white people.

Thought returnin', to me. Will Leavenworth Prison be the same as Indin boardin' schools? Will I disappear into the night? Will I suffer from unwanted touches? I pray to the Creator. Do not let this happen to me again!

Chief spirit words come to me, "Count rivers, states, towns." This I remember. Will I survive Leavenworth?

The half-breed Indin agent and his club, pokin' me in the ribs, yankin' at irons, pushin' me on to the train, sounds of chains draggin' along the narrow train aisle, sendin' shivers up my back. The marshal pointin' his rifle to empty leather seats next to a train window.

Starin' out the train's club window, thinkin' back three moons ago, I was a gatherin', huntin', fishin', feedin' my family, a free man, followin' the Ojibwe way.

Corn! I see fields of corn as the train rumbles pass nearby towns. My thoughts, will I plant Mother Earth's three sister food again. Will I be a farmer again?

Arrivin' in Kansas City, Kansas, lookin' out the train window, I eye prison guards alongside a black government car, letterin' on the door read "Leavenworth Prison."

Long barrel rifles slung over guards shoulders, chains, wrist, leg shackles, clubs, pile in heaps at the train cement platform, waitin for the Indin prisoner.

Steppin' off the train platform, the marshal speaks to law enforcin' guards, "the prisoner, Frank Doolittle, a Wisconsin Indian, ridin' three days on the train, from Madison to Kansas City, Kansas. From here, armed prison guards will transport Frank Doolittle, to a government car and Leavenworth Prison." The marshal removes wrist handcuffs, hands over my conviction papers and states my name as "Frank Doolittle, Inmate bound over to Leavenworth." Guards shackle my arms and legs.

I am seated in the back seat prison car next to the armed guard. My frame of 6'4", there is not much head space. Crouchin' and turnin' my neck I look out the car window. Town people, glarin' back at me, shakin' their heads. Sweat forms on my upper lip, tremblin' with fear, I wonder what awaits me at that Leavenworth Prison.

The government guard drives, hits the open dirt roads, passin' long rows of tall corn, ready for pickin'. The day is warm, bright and clear. Turnin' my eyes to the open fields, watchin' corn stocks, swayin' back and forth in the dry winds of Kansas. Thinkin'. I was once a farmer. Plantin' the three sister, corn, squash, and beans. Will Leavenworth take that livelihood away? Will I stay fit and stay strong? The food! Will I eat sour mush again! Will Leavenworth make me eat diseased livestock and infected flour?

United States Penitentiary Leavenworth, Kansas

Chapter 11

My thoughts return to three months ago, a free man, walkin' freely in the sugar bush, tappin', collectin', and boilin' sap.

George, George Curtis, a brother from Odanah, hearin' him makin' his way through the woodlands, clompin' along on The *Hard Crust of the Snow Moon* carryin' bear snow shoes. He speaks of smellin' a camp fire, seein' smoke risin'. *Eya'*, Frank's in the sugar bush, tappin', a warm day, trees drippin' sap. Talkin', make rounds, emptin' buckets, stickin' dirty fingers into syrup, tastin', laughin', and havin' a good chew.

Eya,' good. We give thanks to Mother Earth for a good harvest.

Afternoon colder. Sap tricklin' into birch bark buckets. Not good.

Eya'! Time to quit! Cold! *Eya'*! A bit thirsty. 'Bout time to sneak a quick drink at Stanley's Saloon. A good long walk from the sugar bush. Just a few miles down the road to Sanborn.

Common sense tells me, it's a crazy notion. The Feds! Would the Feds be there? Watchin' and waitin' for the Indins? We brothers do not want to be caught and thrown in jail buyin' liquor!

March of 1917, the 19th day, George and me, standin' outside Stanley Talaska's Summit Saloon in Sanborn, Wisconsin, on the Bad River Reservation, we met up with our brothers—Fred, Harry, James, and Joe, each wantin' a drink.

Pausin', talkin', and listenin' to Sister School church bells ringin', we speak, "*Eya'*, Sunday mass."

We speak of "needin' a drink again." Our four brothers handin' over coins to fetch whiskey from Stanley. With the coins in our pocket, George Curtis and me, Frank Doolittle, to buy 10 pints of whiskey from Stanley. Our brothers—Fred, Harry, James, and Joe—wait outside in the cold March winds. George and me, steppin' inside the dark large saloon and handin' over the saloon keeper the coins and told him we wanted 10 pints of whiskey.

Our eyes did not adjust well to Stanley's dark saloon. Not seein' the white Federal Indin agent, he place us under arrest, handcuff us on the spot. Seated in the back seat of a government car, we were driven to the Ashland Police Station. Words came to me, Stanley Talaska was fined 50 bucks.

My way of life changed on that day. I was no longer a farmer, a gather, a hunter, or fisher for my people. I was not a free man. I never heard from George Curtis again, or his whereabouts.

May 1917, day 17th, in Madison, Wisconsin. Rememberin' that day, a white judge, yellin', "That Indian is guilty! I'm sentencin' him to Leavenworth Prison, one year and one day! Get that Indian out of my court room!"

I did not understand the Great White Father Washington laws. If only I had a chew. I would say a few words.
Does the judge think I am a dirty drunken Indin!
I am the First People of this country and the government in Washington denies my people U.S. Citizenship.

In the darkest of night, durin' the *Storytelliin' Moon*, a cold December, Father, the Chief Spirit words comes to me. He speaks, "My son, my son, do not despair. You will find your way. You will hunt, fish, gather, and share with your people. Be strong."

This I remember. This I understand.

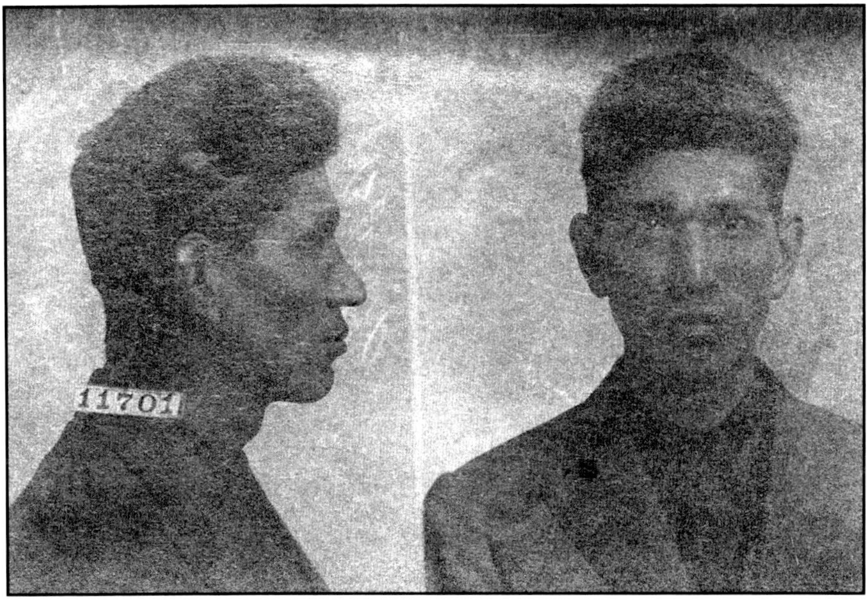

Mug Shot of Frank Doolittle, Inmate 11701
United States Penitentiary Leavenworth

Chapter 12

My eyes takin' notice, high barbed wire stockade outside massive gray rocks. A chill comes over me in this hot July day, a feeling in one's bones, a warning. There is no escape from Leavenworth.

Stretchin' my long neck, to get a closer look, I am told by guards, prisoners built the prison! Free prisoner labor!

Inside the cement block house, I see more guards, cussin' swear words, yellin' military orders, marchin' in dirty army uniforms, long-barrel rifles slung over their slump shoulders. A butt of a gun nudgin', marchin' me forward. A thought comes to mind, five at time marchin' at Odanah, fifteen at Flandreu and eighteen at Carlisle. Now, I am 31, and marchin' at Leavenworth Prison. The Plains Indin, at Carlisle, I hear stories from Lakotas, they say, their ancestors tell stories of many Blue Coats came into their villages with guns, and clubs. Many mothers and Elders died, many children were left without grandmothers. They do not have grandmothers to teach them. Now the government guards wear brown coats.

Thinkin' back to my arrest on April 17, 1917, in Madison, Wisconsin jail, cellmates speak of "United States is at war!" Maybe these Leavenworth guards, their act of marchin' wishin' to be call to service to honor their country. I hear stories at the Madison jail. All Indin males must have a registration card for the war. I do not like war.

My Mary, the mother of my two boys, was born the year of the last Indin war, in the Sioux Nation. Carlisle was at war with the Indin children, destroyin' them with their clubs, beatin' them, feeding them rancid livestock, poor grains. Many were left behind at the Carlisle cemetery. Never to be return to their people. Will Leavenworth be the same?

My mind slippin' back, the ride to Leavenworth in the government car. I made no talk, do not eye guards. Listenin' to them with open ears, they speak of Leavenworth, the drunken Indin's new home. The Indin will work rock pile, makin' bricks, haulin', buildin' new prison cells for more Indin prisoners. There's more talk, a sawmill at the prison. *Eya'*, sawmill I hear. I once work at the Stearns Sawmill in Sanborn, maybe I could work the sawmill in prison. I will ask. The guards ramble on about the prison, the barns, a baker, a tailor, and shoe shop. I think it over. *Eya'*, I am in need of haircut, a new set of clothin', and good leather shoes.

Guards lock me in heavy chains, pushin'me along dark narrow tunnels, chains draggin' and scrapin' on wet cement floor, the sound, an eerie feelin's in my body, like a death march to a cell. Will I ever leave this prison? Will the guards bury me in a dirt mound? Will the prison have a Catholic mass? Thoughts of it leave me cold rememberin' the Catholic Masses at Indin boardin' schools. The priest, nuns, and white Indin agents, they say, it is their God! Indin children must be saved from their wicked ways. The savages will be punish, beaten, and learn' the Christian teachin'!

Walkin' in the dark tunnel, above me, slight shakin', turnin' my head and lookin' to the guard, he tells me, "Buildings old, machinery and convicts on upper floors. Floors will give way soon. You'll just be another dead Indian."

A small window ahead gives more light. The door lettering reads: Tailor Shop. *Eya'*, this is where I will wear new clothin'. Bendin' my head to enter the room my head looks down over a short, scrawny clean shaven man. A squawkin' voice tells me, "will fit you with a shirt, tie, and suit coat." Wrist and leg irons are cuttin' into my flesh, the guard grins, and does not remove the shackles for the tailors fittin'. *Eya'* if only I had a good chew, to take my mind away from the pain.

The guard's club motionin' me to another door, a sign reads: Barber Shop. The barber, he speaks of a "haircut and a shave for inmate 11707." He smells of tobacco and whiskey. Pickin' up leg chains and takin' a seat into the torn leather cushion, the iron weights off my feet, chains are loose and do not dig into my torn flesh. The barber takes a long scissor to my thick black hair. Grumblin' and gruntin' he speaks of me as dirty Indin and havin' lice. This Indin has no facial hair. No shave.

Walkin' to another well-lit large room a short, scrawny man speaks, he takes pictures. He must be less than 100 pounds soakin' wet, his skin taut, hardly enough to cover his bones. Maybe has not seen enough day light. The ill-fittin' clothin' he wears, soil, smells of sweat, tobacco, and whiskey.

He'd best see the prison tailor. Not enough wages at Leavenworth to speak of. He speaks of takin' a mug shot. I am told the President, Woodrow Wilson of the United States, wants all convicts mug shots printable. I am to sit and not move. Number 11707 is sewn into the prisoner's coat collar. A guard barks orders, inmate need shoes for the rock pile!

The heat of summer, my skin cold, clammy, flashes of light cross my eyes, weaken me. I need to breathe, to rest. The weight leg irons become heavier, I struggle with each step.

Countin' cement grey brick the tunnel is old and in need of much repair. Feelin' the shakin' from above, I take notice of iron braces holding up the ceilin'. Dampness, leakin' pipes and the smell of slop pails makin' it difficult to breath.

From behind, hearin' heavy breathin, inmates gruntin' drunken Indin talk, and laughin', mockin' me.
It is best I remain silent and look down to my feet.

Hobblin' along on each foot, the club nudgin' into my shoulder. Feelin' terror, my body stricken's with a cold sweat. Will the club make a blow into my back? Stumblin', fallin' on knees and arms, crawlin' like a dog to lift myself upright, the noose, tightin' around my neck. I gasp for breath. My neck! Did I break my neck?

Maple Sugar Moon, the day of the arrest, I once stood straight as an arrow— 6' 4." Held my head high, had a strong arm grip, could outrun the fastest bear and snare many of rabbits. Splittin', choppin', clearin' woodlands for to make ready for plowin', plantin' come spring, the three sister plants, corn, squash, and beans. *Eya'*, a good harvest will come.

Soon, it is July, the *Halfway Through the Summer Moon*, berry pickin' time. The body aches. Weights of irons, pullin' on shoulders, ankles and neck, cuttin' into my loose flesh. Shoulder slumpin' forward, the back curvin and the neck droppin' forward. I am no longer straight as an arrow.

Feelin' like a dead man, walkin' through a dim lit tunnel, the guard, he speaks of a shortcut, as the crow flies. His eyes watchin' me from behind, the club begin shovin' and draggin me to Cell Block 322 at Leavenworth Prison.
It is May 17, the year of 1917.

The silence and waitin' becomes unbearable. Smellin' him from behind me, waitin'. Making a loud gruntin' sound, he's slappin' the club against the palm of his beefy hands, waitin'. I feel his eyes borin' into my neck, the hair stands on ends, sendin' shivers down my back. I dare not move, wonderin' when the next blow will come. He removes the irons and walks slowly to the steel door, turnin' and shovin' me forward, slammin' the iron door shut.

Stumblin' on my feet, a cough comes from the belly, spittin' up thick brown foam. Thinkin' to myself, I have the white man's disease, T.B., the plague. Chief *Osaguie* of Wisconsin Point speaks of the plague in 1916. Many of my village people had journin' on to the spirit word from this plague. The white man plague.

Tremblin', dizziness, unsteadiness is takin' over my body. My arms reachin' out, needin' somethin' to steady myself. Strainin' the eyes, spottin' a rusted metal bed, a straw mattress, a small pox blanket, and in the corner, a slop pail, overflowin' with body waste. Unthinkin', my right hand touches my face. Blood! Blood from my ears!

Shufflin' to the beam of light, a small window with bars high to the ceilin'. Thinkin' to myself, does that guard count on me escapin' through that window? Stretchin' I let the sun rays warm my thin worn body. Weak and wastin' skin and bones, the belly aches from hunger, a skeleton of a man. The July sun, slowly slippin' behind dark clouds, maybe rain will come. I feel bad spirits enterin' this dark dungeon, the guard calls cell block 322.

Hearin' noise, turnin' around, callers! Rats! Rats in cell 322, dartin' behind the slop pail, runnin' into holes in the cement bricks. I have no food for them. Tomorrow, sneakin' prison food, feed rats, and watch them get sick.
This I will do.

Beddin' down, I cover myself with the thin small pox blanket, lookin' up at peelin' paint, thinkin' out loud about the white man's crime laws. Learnin' to read, write, and add at Indin boardin'schools, I will write and ask Chief Buffalo people to write our own reservation laws.
I will ask for paper and ink. This is what I will do.

I am an old man of 31, tired, worn out and in need of a nap. A nap will do me good while I think about the white government laws against the Indins.

A loud grunt startles me. The guard, lookin' down at me, a sneer coverin' his beef red face. I did not hear him enter cell 322. I must think of a plan to warn me of his next approach. The club moves up and down the metal bed frame, the sounds frightenin' me, sendin shivers down my back. Freezin' in fear, I make no sound. I dare not let the guard know how I fear him.

The guards club pointin' to the iron bar door, he shovin' and hittin' my knees from behind. I buckle under. Stabbin' pain brought me down on all fours. The guard, I see it his, face he enjoys watchin' me. Grimacin', I remain silent.
I have not had this much pain since Carlisle Indin Boarding School.

I hear a crack. Takin' notice, I look at my feet, puddles of blood form on the cement floor. The club, points to a cat walk. I slowly upright myself, thinkin' to myself, I suffer in pain at Leavenworth for buyin' whiskey on my reservation.

I do not know the white man's laws. Standin', bearin' down on each foot, pain shootin' up and down the legs. Walkin' and pushin' forward with each step, a path of bloody footprints follow me from behind. With despair, thoughts return of blood memories at Indin boarding school.

Thinkin' to myself, I will spend years in Leavenworth and never see my clan people again. I shudder at the thought.

Security devices from
United States Penitentiary
Leavenworth, Kansas

Chapter 13

From behind me, the guard speaks, mutterin'. "The Army doctor to see you! You know, the convicts built Leavenworth prison hospital, free labor from the rock pile!"

Leaving Cell block 322, walkin' through cell block after cell block, seein', hearin' convicts sneerin', Indin war whoops, yelpin' like sick dogs, "Indian, who did you scalp?
A drunken Indian! Speak English, Indian?"

Keepin' my head low, almost touchin' my chest, eyes fix on my swollen bloody feet. Limpin' with each step, the painful sore spots are like hot ashes burin' into open wounds. I do not make a sound, my eyes and face remains blank. Side of my eye, I take notice, hollow blank eyes staring back at me. *Eya'*, white inmates, the war haters, their hands drawn tightly to cell doors, their feet barely touching the floor.
I hear, the war haters have bread and water for days.
I am a war hater, but with a cough. The army only wants able-bodies men and I am not a U.S. citizen.

The guard, like a devil in one's side, laughin', slammin' his club against the iron bars, an eerie breakin' noise.

A force of air escapes from my lungs coughin' and throwin' up brown foam from the mouth landin' on the dirty cement floor. Convicts stop laughin' and back away from the cell bars, the guard steps back, his club touchin' my back.

Thinkin' to myself, this cough I have, this white man's cough, I will speak to the Army doctor. Do I have the white man's disease? T.B.? The plague? Chief *Osagie*, a headman from Wisconsin Point, speaks of a vision in 1916, "There will be a Plague."

This Army doctor exam room must be a good way off, maybe on the other side of the prison. A long walk in dark tunnel for me, irons heavy with weights, and the guard, will he strike a blow? The ankles skin is torn, openin' with blood. The neck yoke is pullin' my neck down. Gray brick walls appear to be closin' in on me. Then there's a tight narrow walkway. I need a little fresh air, stuffy, hard to breathe. Do I gamble, take a chance and ask the guard for a rest? It's best that I remain silent.

The prison guard whacks his club into my back, pushin' me toward a door. A sign on the door reads: Army Doctor Exam Room. The club knocks on the closed door. Standin' inside the room, a white Army doctor speaks his name–Dr. Tyole. Inmate 11701, Frank Doolittle. The guard unlocks the shackles. A heavy burden is removed. Now, I stand straight as an arrow, 6'4."

My eyes remain fixed on the little man, takin' notice. His eyes are hollow and blank, long thin fingers, tightly drawn brownish-yellow face. He must not have seen the light of day for some time. Dr. Tyole askin' the question of me. "Do you speak English?" Noddin' my head, I answer yes to each question he asks.

Frank Doolittle, Age 31;
Catholic Schooling–grade 4; Indian; married 2 times; children–2 boys; farmer; chews; smokes; drinks; crimes against the government.

The army doctor examines me, talkin' to himself, "Inmate 11701, 6' 2 ½, weight 150; left wrist injury, flesh open. Right hand bleedin', flesh open, nose canal broken, teeth crushed, back bruisin', lice nestin' in thick hair. Eyes puffy, bruisin' on facial cheeks." "How did you get these injuries?" Bowin' my head to the floor, remainin' silent.

Smellin' his presence behind me, the guard eyes bearin' down into my neck, I hear his club slappin' into the palm of his hand. The doctor asks again, "How did these injuries happen?" Flinchin', tremblin', and shruggin' my shoulders with fear, I say nothin'.

Crumblin' over with a cough, spillin' up brown foam, the doctor asks, "Who coughs in your family? How many months have you coughed?" I answer, "My mother, she coughs." The doctor tells the guard, "Inmate Frank Doolittle, 11701, has T.B. Confine him to Hospital Quarantine with light duty." Thinkin' to myself, what is "light duty?" I have the white man plague, T.B.

The guard, shovin' his club into my back, grumblin', leadin' me through steel doors, to the quarantine hospital. Leavin' behind at the doctor's exam room, a heap of iron chains.

Thinkin' to myself, why does the guard not lock me in those irons? *Eya'*, but the feelin' is good, breathin' more easily, freedom from those weights. I will manage to walk with no limp.

Keepin' a safe distance from me, the guard, my thoughts are he fears he will get the plague from me. The white man's T.B. A short walk to a large wooden double door with a metal plague that reads "Quarantine Hospital."

The guard points for me to open the wide entry door and enter the hospital. My thoughts return to my youth, an old Indin hospital next to boarding school, smellin' of white man's remedies. This Quarantine Hospital smells of white medicine. Healin' plants for T.B.? These white doctors do not know how to heal. They do not use the four healing plants. Their medicine burns my broken nose and chest. I take to a heavy cough. The guard, backs away from me. I have mind to turn and cough on that bully.

A sudden effort to breath, coughin' from deep inside my lungs, causes me to remember, the *Rising Moon* of 1916, Chief *Osagie*, a headman from Wisconsin Point comes to our village. He speak loud, Ojibwe tongue, "A steel works company is taking our burial land and digging up our ancestors. This nation will visit a terrible fire, a plague and war! I have spoken!"

Eya' this is a sizable room, this hospital. Large windows will be good. There is much sunlight.

The Army doctor, he writes, "Frank Doolittle will not be sent to the rock pile, assigned to light duty." A hospital guard, an Army nurse, he tells me of light duty, an orderly, keepin' the hospital tidy, clean, in order and helpin' the T.B. patients.

"Do you understand English?" Noddin' yes, I remain silent. The white doctors kept me in Quarantine Hospital for 3 months on light duty. Scrubbin' floors, laundry, feedin', bathin' T.B. patients, emptyin' slop pails, washin' dishes, and keepin' the hospital tidy.

Durin' the hospital stay, Leavenworth billed me for daily dressin' changes, dental expenses, food allowances, clothing, foot wear, and haircuts. This was taken out of my $7,000 allotment monies.

With a keen eye, takin' notice of the white Army nurses, they look to be well fed and able bodied and not eatin' with or the same food as the T.B. patients. Sneakin' a look into a mirror, my face was the color of death, sickly, wastin' away to skin and bones. The white medicine did not stop my cough. Shakin' off that fear, eating' the prison mush, putting 'meat on my bones I think, I rid myself of the white man's cough. This I will do.

Two years passin' since I heard of Chief *Osagie's* vision. At Leavenworth Quarantine Hospital word came to the prisoners, American and the Old Countries at war. *Osagie's* plague, T.B., is spreading around the U.S. country!

Prisoners marching at United States Penitentiary Leavenworth.

Chapter 14

In the fourth month at Quarantine Hospital, a white Army doctor speaks, "Frank Doolittle, Inmate 11707, is healthy enough to work the farm, teamsters, and prison stables." I am to plow the fields again. I am to be a farmer again. I am to be a Teamster. I do know their words, a teamster. Boardin' school did not teach me English words pass grade four. The guards put me, the drunken Indin in charge of haulin' supply wagons with a team of horses, to farm fields, rock piles, brick yards, and barns. They keep their distance, away from me, I still have the cough.

The prison guards took pleasure, watchin me cleanin' the prison stable, haulin' hay bales, shovelin' horse manure onto a buck wagon, waterin', feedin', shoein' team of Leavenworth draft horses.

Guards laughin', makin' Indin jokes, knowin' I do not speak out. Wonderin' to myself, in the last Indin War, did the guards have family that fought with the Lakota and wore Blue Coats. A blank look I have on my face, I make no talk. The guards, they call me a dumb Indian. The guards, do not know, my spirits are high, workin' the stables and not the rock pile.

The spring of 1918, eight months into my prison sentence, the Warden Office sent word to me, that inmate 11707, Frank Doolittle, cell block 322, will be workin' for Warden Thomas W. Morgan as a stable boy, groomin', feedin', waterin', harnessin' his prize draft horses. Remainin' silent, I wonder to myself, does Warden Morgan treat his horses with kindness better than his Leavenworth prisoners?

July 1918, *Halfway Through the Summer Moon*, berry pickin' time. At first light, cell block 322 iron gate opens. A trusty prisoner I am, inmate 11707, no longer wearin' iron chains, the bully guard pokes his club into my back walkin' me to Warden Morgan prized draft horses. I do not fear his club, the guard will not, the warden stable boy, cause injury to my body. Early daybreak, the hot dry Kansas winds pickin' up, tastin' blowin' dust in my mouth, causin' a cough. Will this cough never leave me? Leavenworth prison did not rid me of the white T.B disease. Will I carry this cough back to my people?

Soon, Warden Morgan a man of fine breedin', will make his presence at Leavenworth stables, gentle taps, leadin' the biggest mares to the waterin' trough, strokin', brushin', whisperin' and hand feedin' them sugary treats. I wonder to myself, a man of fine breedin', why he is not gentle with inmates of Leavenworth Prison. Ojibwe Indin inmate 11707, Warden Morgan stable boy, handin' over leather reins to the warden, watchin' him ridin' across the open fields. Rememberin' my earlier thoughts, *eya'*, the warden treats his horses with kindness.

I count days, July 23, 1918, I will be released from Leavenworth Prison for good behavior. My last day at the stables, to watch Warden Morgan ride his prize stallions.

Chapter 15

Squirmin' into a hollow oak trunk, the fourth day of freedom, my bony hands come to rest on a few wild mushrooms. Thinkin', *eya'* safe to eat, ready for pickin'. Bend stiff fingers pickin' the biggest. Brushin' aside dirt, takin' small bite, swallowin' slowly. *Eya'*, tasty.

The corner of my eye spots movements. Worms!
Poppin' of brown heads, wormin' their way through the dirt. Thoughts enter my head. If I was closer to shoreline, a willow stick, a handful of worms, I would make a snare and start a small fire. I would catch a big walleye, take only what I could eat and give *Migizi* a treat. This is the Ojibwe way.

The day begins with the risin' sun, branches shadin' the dense woodlands, hushin' of pine trees, quietness surroundin' me. Scentin' my Father, the Chief, and Mother; they are near.

Lookin' eastward to the shores, Mother Earth's familiar path, followin' the trail many times in the past, between tall pines leadin' to my village. Chantin' Ojibwe travelin' songs. Followin my ancestors walk, they will guide, heal, feed, and make my broken body strong again.
I will walk the courage of life.

Migizi he flies high above the pines, circlin', droppin' his gift, his feather. Reachin' over with my right arm, crushin' pain sets me recoilin'.

Crooked fingers touchin' his gift, pickin' it up slowly, gently layin' the feather across my chest. Closin' my eyes, givin' a *Miigwech*. *Migizi's* gift will help me walk the path to healin'.

Takin' one step at a time, each foot bringin' me closer to my people. Forgettin' my footin', I'm tumblin' over a sizable willow trunk, and takin' a fall on a soft bed of needles.

Spread-eagle on my back, a lapse of time set me back. The *Freezing Water Moon*, the year of 1905 at the Bad River Reservation. I'm eighteen, a run-a-way from Carlisle Indian School. Walking the same familiar path, followin' Father, the Chief, *mindimooyag*, hunters, mothers without children, holding babies.

No school-age children are about. I do not speak. I know. They were taken by government agents and forced into Catholic Indin boardin' school, thousands of miles from the Bad River Reservation. *Eya'*, they suffer as I suffered at the white Catholic boardin' schools. My heart fillin' with heavy sorrow for lost children, and there is nothin' I can do.

My mind is strayin'. Mother is not beside her husband, my father, the Chief James Doolittle. The wise man takin' notice of my thoughts, he speaks, "Your Mother has journey on to the spirit world."

Thirteen year later, the Catholic Indin boarding school agents still come into our village and take our children. My sons, Joseph and Fred, I hear from my clan people, they speak of beatin', empty bellies, alone. They do not speak or look into white eyes.

Feelin' a brush of a hand, large strong hands, Father pushin' me to rise, stand on my feet. Fingers lightly stroke my right arm. Warmth comes to my bones, a feelin' of no longer hurtin'.

Gently, my father picks me up and guides me to my feet, wrappin' big arms around me. I am standin' straight as an arrow, shoulders no longer slouchin' forward. Bleedin' in the right arm has stoppin'. A feeling of warmth is overtakin' my body. Thirst and hunger no longer in my belly.
A diamond willow stick steadies my long thin legs.
I'm walkin' at a good pace.

A short distance lookin' to the east, smoke risin' above the pines, the smell of wood burnin', clan people buildin' fires, a feast is waitin' at the long house. *Eya'*, smellin' fry bread, deer meat, and rice. My people, they wait.

Father, the Chief, and Mother are beside me.

I am no longer alone.

Epilogue

Shortly after Frank Doolittle ran away from Carlisle, an Indian ceremony took place on the Bad River Reservation. In 1906 my grandfather married my grandmother, Mary Houle, from the Fond du Lac Reservation. After having two boys, the marriage ended in annulment in 1914. Four months later, grandfather remarried, another marriage ending in annulment. His first wife Mary fetched him from Bad River, knowing he had tuberculosis and brought him to Fond du Lac Rez, and nursed him for three years. He journeyed on in 1922.

The story telling I heard from my brother Fred tells of the boys, forced to attend Catholic Indian Boarding School in Hayward, Wisconsin. At that time they were ages 9 and 13. My brother speaks of the two boys sending word to their mother on the Fond du Lac Rez, "Father is sick–go and get him!"

This left me with lingering questions: Did Grandfather somehow send word to his boys that he was sick with a cough? Did he make his presence in the dark of night while the boys slept, to speak of his illness? Did he drop a feather?

In the Native culture, we sense things happening, perhaps a vision, a presence of another person. We listen, sometimes with feelings so strong we give tobacco and pray to the Creator.

There are many different stories like my grandfather's to be shared. Each one reminds us of the wrongs and devastation of the Indian boarding school, the assault on Native cultural identity. The inherited pain of the cultural genocide that is still carried in the faces and the walks of our people today. The memories of pain, suffering from physical, mental, and sexual abuse are passed down through generations as blood memories.

Many stories are told and retold and each one is important.

Frank Doolittle Timeline

1886 - Born in Houghton, Michigan, May 28, 1886, to James and Mary Rose Doolittle.

1891-1901 - In 1891, at age 5, Frank Doolittle is forcibly taken from his northern reservation home to his first boarding school at Odanah, Wisconsin.

1901-1905 - Flandreau Indian School (Boarding School), Flandreau, South Dakota.

1905 - Carlisle Indian Industrial School (Boarding School), Carlisle, Pennsylvania. (Runaway after 1 month)

1917-1918 - In 1917, at age 31, he is arrested on the reservation for buying liquor and sent to the United States Penitentiary at Leavenworth, Kansas.

1922 - Died of Pulmonary Tuberculosis on October 6,1922. Buried at Fond du Lac Reservation Holy Family Catholic Church, Cloquet, Minnesota.

Mary Houle Doolittle, first wife of Frank Doolittle, and Fred Doolittle Sr., son of Mary and Frank, c. 1922

Joseph and Fred Doolittle, sons of Frank and Mary Houle Doolittle

Documents

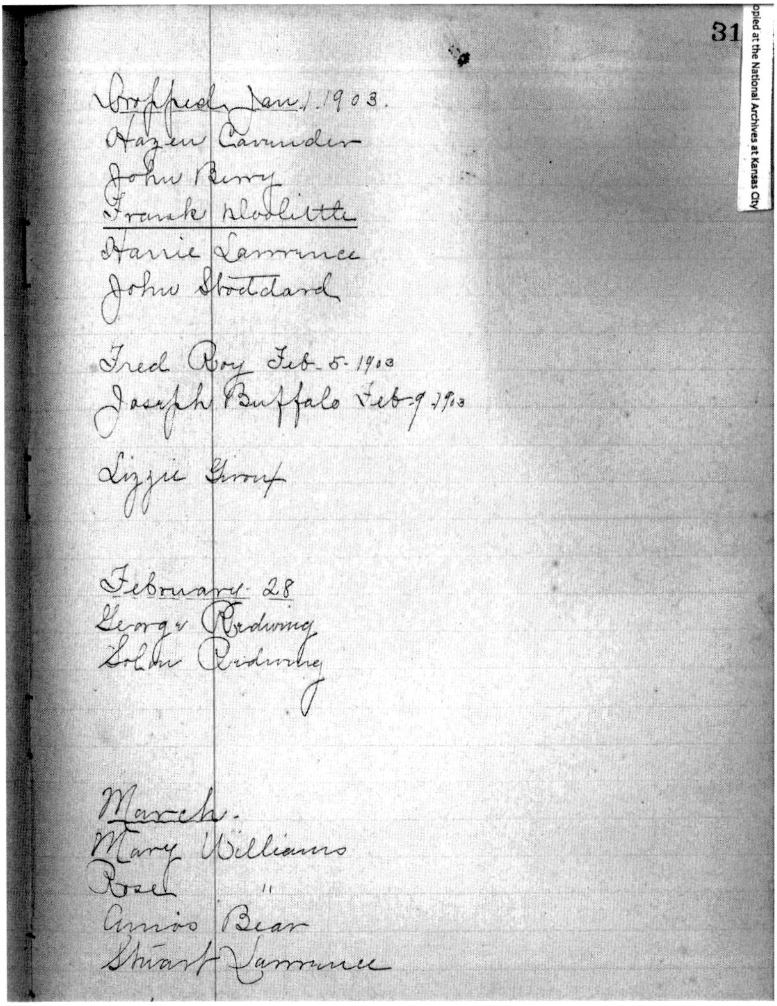
31

opied at the National Archives at Kansas City

Dropped Jan 1. 1903.
Hazen Cavender
John Berry
Frank Doolittle

Harrie Lawrence
John Stoddard

Fred Roy Feb. 5. 1903
Joseph Buffalo Feb. 9. 1903

Lizzie Groof

February 28
George Redwing
Solon Redwing

March.
Mary Williams
Rose "
Amos Bear
Stuart Lawrence

Records of Frank Doolittle's enrollment from the *Franciscan Sisters of Perpetual Adoration School* in Odanah, Wisconsin.

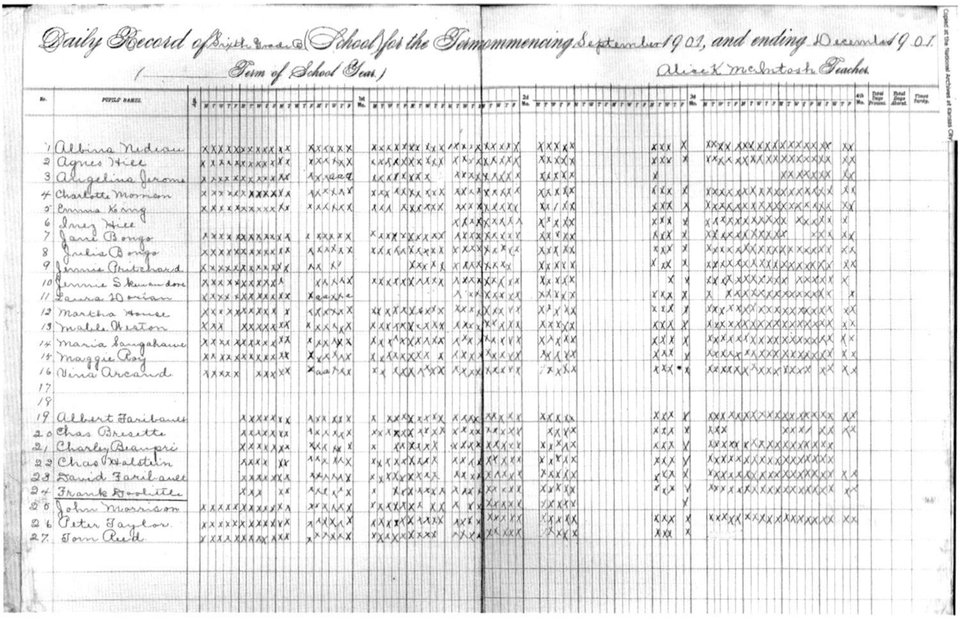
Daily Record of Sixth Grade (School) for the Term commencing September 1901, and ending December 1901.
(Term of School Year.)
Alice K McIntosh Teacher

No.	Pupils' Names
1	Albina Nideau
2	Agnes Hill
3	Angelina Jerome
4	Charlotte Morrison
5	Emma King
6	Inez Hill
7	Jane Bongo
8	Julia Bongo
9	Jennie Pritchard
10	Jennie Skenandore
11	Laura Dorian
12	Martha House
13	Mable Heston
14	Maria Sangahaw
15	Maggie Roy
16	Vina Arcand
17	
18	
19	Albert Fairbanks
20	Chas Bresette
21	Charley Beaupri
22	Chas Halstein
23	David Fairbanks
24	Frank Doolittle
25	John Morrison
26	Peter Taylor
27	Tom Reed

Records of Frank Doolittle's enrollment from the *Franciscan Sisters of Perpetual Adoration School* in Odanah, Wisconsin.

423

APPLICATION FOR ENROLLMENT IN A NON-RESERVATION SCHOOL.

Full name of child Frank S Doolittle Indian name ______
______ Name of father, Jim Doolittle Name of Mother, Mary Doolittle Tribe, Chippewa Reservation, Bad River Degree of Indian blood of child, half.
Is either parent white, if so, which? No ______ Are either or both allotted? Both On what reservation? Bad River
Age of child 19 What reservation school attended, Catholic & Public
When, and how long, 7 years If ever enrolled in a non-reservation school, Flandreau S.D. When, 1901 How long? 1903
If ever dismissed from school, where ______ when, ______ and for what reason ______

Frank S Doolittle.

Consent Blank.

I, Frank S Doolittle Parent, guardian of the above named child, ______ do hereby consent to the transfer or enrollment for a period of ~~five~~ (3) years in the Indian School at Carlisle, Pa.
Dated at Odanah Wis. on the 29 day of Aug. 1905 - 1905.

Frank S Doolittle.

~~AGENT~~

Physician's Certificate.

I hereby certify that I have personally examined the above named Frank Doolittle and have found him phyisically sound and recommend the transfer so far as his health, conditions are concerned.
Dated at Odanah on the 30 day of Aug 1905.

William J. Griffin
Agency Physician

AGENTS ENDORSEMENT

Aug. 31st 1905.

The statement concerning above named Frank S Doolittle are believed by me to be correct, and I hereby recommend the transfer.

S.W. Campbell
U.S. Ind. Agt.

Name Frank Doolittle | File No. En. " " G. 423 " " D.
Indian name
Tribe Chippewa Age 18 Blood
Agency La Pointe Wis.
Father James Doolittle
Arrived 9-5-05 Departed 10-24-05 Cause Deserter
Class entered 4th Class left 4th
Trade Outing
Character
Married Deceased
Remarks over
YAWMAN & ERBE MFG. CO., ROCHESTER, N. Y. 817915 8M 6-10

Forms from Carlisle Indian Industrial School, Carlisle, Pennsylvania.

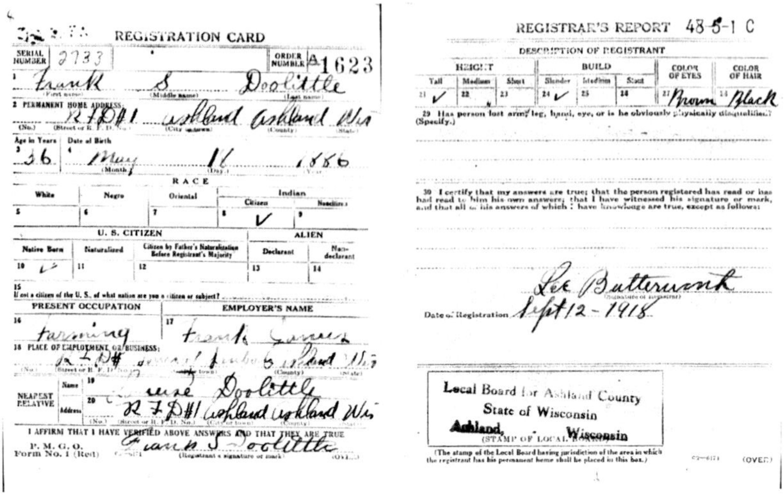

REGISTRATION CARD

SERIAL NUMBER 2733 | ORDER NUMBER A1623

1 Frank S Doolittle (First name) (Middle name) (Last name)

2 PERMANENT HOME ADDRESS: R F D #1 Ashland Ashland Wis (No.) (Street or R. F. D. No.) (City or town) (County) (State)

Age in Years 36 | Date of Birth May 11 1886 (Month) (Day) (Year)

RACE

White	Negro	Oriental	Indian: Citizen	Indian: Noncitizen
5	6	7	8 ✓	9

U. S. CITIZEN: Native Born	Naturalized	Citizen by Father's Naturalization Before Registrant's Majority	ALIEN: Declarant	Non-declarant
10 ✓	11	12	13	14

15 If not a citizen of the U. S., of what nation are you a citizen or subject?

PRESENT OCCUPATION: 16 farming | EMPLOYER'S NAME: 17 Frank Jones

18 PLACE OF EMPLOYMENT OR BUSINESS: R F D# ... Ashland Wis

NEAREST RELATIVE: Name 19 Louise Doolittle | Address 20 R F D #1 Ashland Ashland Wis

I AFFIRM THAT I HAVE VERIFIED ABOVE ANSWERS AND THAT THEY ARE TRUE

P. M. G. O. Form No. 1 (Red) Frank S Doolittle (Registrant's signature or mark)

REGISTRAR'S REPORT 48-5-1 C

DESCRIPTION OF REGISTRANT

Height: Tall	Medium	Short	Build: Slender	Medium	Stout	Color of Eyes	Color of Hair
21 ✓	22	23	24 ✓	25	26	27 Brown	28 Black

29 Has person lost arm, leg, hand, eye, or is he obviously physically disqualified? (Specify.)

30 I certify that my answers are true; that the person registered has read or has had read to him his own answers; that I have witnessed his signature or mark, and that all of his answers of which I have knowledge are true, except as follows:

Lee Butterwork (Signature of registrar)

Date of Registration Sept 12 - 1918

Local Board for Ashland County State of Wisconsin Ashland, Wisconsin (STAMP OF LOCAL BOARD)

(The stamp of the Local Board having jurisdiction of the area in which the registrant has his permanent home shall be placed in this box.)

(OVER)

Frank Doolittle's World War I Draft Registration.

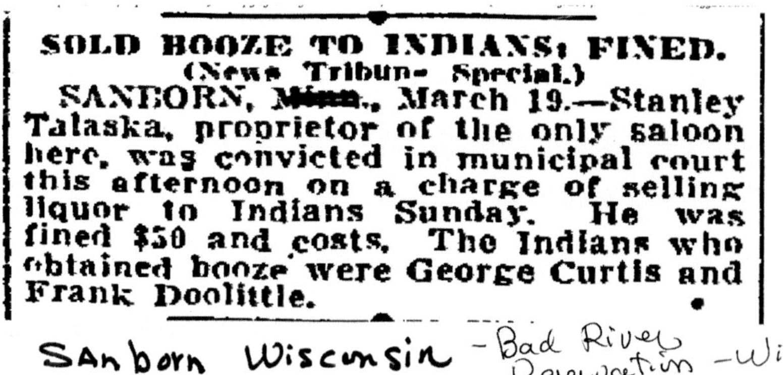

SOLD BOOZE TO INDIANS; FINED.

(News Tribune Special.)

SANBORN, Minn., March 19.—Stanley Talaska, proprietor of the only saloon here, was convicted in municipal court this afternoon on a charge of selling liquor to Indians Sunday. He was fined $50 and costs. The Indians who obtained booze were George Curtis and Frank Doolittle.

The *Duluth News Tribune* article about Frank Doolittle's arrest in Sanborn, Wisconsin. The town is part of the Bad River Reservation and is misidentified in the article as being in Minnesota.

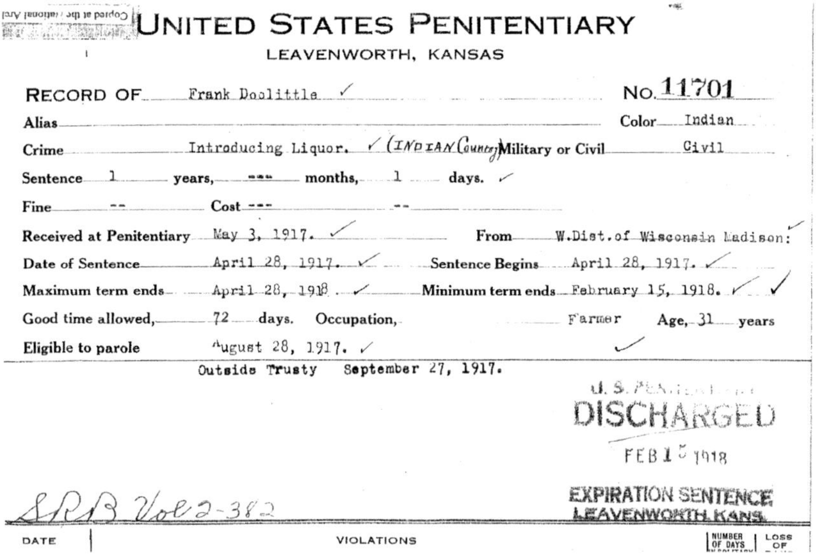
Copied at the National Archives

UNITED STATES PENITENTIARY
LEAVENWORTH, KANSAS

RECORD OF Frank Doolittle ✓ No. 11701

Alias

Color Indian

Crime Introducing Liquor. ✓ (INDIAN Country) Military or Civil Civil

Sentence 1 years, --- months, 1 days. ✓

Fine -- Cost --- --

Received at Penitentiary May 3, 1917. ✓ From W.Dist.of Wisconsin Madison: ✓

Date of Sentence April 28, 1917. ✓ Sentence Begins April 28, 1917. ✓

Maximum term ends April 28, 1918. ✓ Minimum term ends February 15, 1918. ✓ ✓

Good time allowed, 72 days. Occupation, Farmer Age, 31 years

Eligible to parole August 28, 1917. ✓ ✓

Outside Trusty September 27, 1917.

U. S. PENITENTIARY
DISCHARGED
FEB 15 1918
EXPIRATION SENTENCE
LEAVENWORTH, KANS.

SRB Vol 2-382

DATE	VIOLATIONS	NUMBER OF DAYS	LOSS OF

Frank Doolittle Record from United States Penitentiary, Leavenworth, Kansas.

United States of America, } SS.
WESTERN DISTRICT OF WISCONSIN

11701

The President of the United States of America:

To the Marshal of the Western District of Wisconsin, and to the Warden of the United States Penitentiary, Leavenworth, Kansas.

Whereas, Frank Doolittle has been, by the District Court of the United States for the Western District of Wisconsin, convicted of the offense of Introducing liquor onto Indian Reservation in violation of Section 2139 of the U. S. Revised Statutes, and has been sentenced by said Court to imprisonment for One year and one day in the United States Penitentiary, Leavenworth, Kansas, ~~and to pay a fine of $~~ ~~to the United States~~

Sentence to commence at 12 M. of the date hereof.

You, the said Marshal, are hereby commanded forthwith to deliver into the custody of the said United States Penitentiary, Leavenworth, Kansas, the body of Frank Doolittle and you, the said Warden of the United States Penitentiary, Leavenworth, Kansas, are hereby required to receive the said Frank Doolittle into your custody, in the said United States Penitentiary, and him there safely keep, until the expiration of said term of imprisonment, or until he shall be otherwise discharged according to law.

Witness, the Honorable Arthur L. Sanborn, Judge of the District Court of the United States for the Western District of Wisconsin, at the City of Madison, in said District, this 28th day of April in the year of our Lord one thousand nine hundred and seventeen and of the Independence of the United States the one hundred and forty-first.

Attest; F. W. Oakley
Clerk.
By Fred W French
Deputy.

F. W. Oakley, (L. S.)
Clerk.
By Fred W. French,
Deputy.

13

Copied at the National Archives

TRUSTY PRISONER'S AGREEMENT

Name Frank Doolittle, *Number* 11701, *Color* Indian

Crime Introducing Liquor

Sentence, One *years*, *months*, One *days*

Date of Sentence Apr. 28, 1917, *Sent from* W.D.Wisconsin, Madison

Full term expires Apr. 28, 1918, *Short time expires* Feb. 15, 1918

Received at Penitentiary May 3, 1917, *Occupation* Farmer, *Age* 31

Reasons for being made a Trusty prisoner

Is the above-stated name your right name? Yes

If not, what is your right name?

Give a full history of the crime for which you were sent here. It is alleged that I introduced liquor on an Indian Reservation. I plead Guilty
(State fully the nature of the crime. Persons injured physically, financially or otherwise. State when and where the crime was committed. Names of persons with you when the crime was committed and what was done with him or them. State the reason why the crime was committed and whether or not you pleaded guilty at the trial.)

Where and by whom were you arrested? Ashland, Wis. Deputy Sheriff

Are you married? Yes *Number of children?* two

Name and P. O. address of parents Both dead

Name and address of wife Mrs Frank Doolittle, Odanah, Wis.

Have you ever served sentence in Penitentiary, Reformatory, Work House or Jail before? Same. About 1907. Madison, Wis. Jail (3 mo,)
(State under what name, when and where.)

Do you own any real estate? 80 A. Ashland, Wis. $7000.00 Allotment 80 A.
(State where located and the value of it.)

In consideration of being made a Trusty prisoner, I, Frank Doolittle *Number* 11701, *a prisoner in the United States Penitentiary, Leavenworth, Kansas, do hereby pledge my word that I will not attempt to escape from said Penitentiary or Penitentiary Reservation, and will serve faithfully the unexpired part of my sentence.*

(Signature) F. S. Doolittle *Reg. No.* 11701

Remarks: P.S.Everest
P.S.Edwards, Indian Agnt. Ashland, Wis.
F.B.Lamoreux, Atty. Ashland

Frank Doolittle Records from United States Penitentiary, Leavenworth, Kansas.

February 19, 1918.

A/C 11701

Lieut. Raymond G. Barnett,
177 Brig. Headquarters,
Camp Funston, Kansas.

11701

Dear Sir:

I am in receipt of your letter of February 18th in which you state that through mistake an exchange of grips was made by you and Frank S. Doolittle, while you were on the train en route from Camp Funston to Kansas City, and requesting what information I can give you in regard to this party. In reply I will say that Frank S. Doolittle was an inmate of this Penitentiary up till February 15th, on which day he was released. Doolittle was furnished with transportation to Ashland, Wisconsin, and I believe you can communicate with him by directing your letters to him at Route 1, Ashland, Wisconsin. I hope that you will have no difficulty in securing the return of your grip.

Respectfully,

TWM-RM

Warden.

A letter about the "grip" incident on Frank's trip home from Leavenworth.

Notes and Sources

Chapter 1

- Spirits: The Creator Helpers
- Calendar Moons: The *Anishinaabeg* people follow the 13 moons, but most cycles follow the 12 month calendar. The Ojibwe designated the names of the moon to correspond with the season's influence within a given location.
- *Anishinabe*: Ojibwe-American Indian
- Congress passed laws during the 19th century to increase federal control over Indians on reservation and to prosecute. Outlawed: *pow wows*, feasting, liquor, buying, selling, drinking, and must have permission to leave reservation.
  Source: Stephen L. Prevar, *The Rights of Indian and Tribes, 4th ed.*, Oxford University Press, 2012.
- Chippewa Bad River Reservation, Wisconsin: 1854–1200 acre high quality wetlands, wild rice along the Lake Superior's south shore. This area sustained the Ojibwe for generations.
  The settlement: *Odanah*-Ojibwe word for village.
  Source: Patty Loew, *Indian Nations of Wisconsin*, Wisconsin Historical Society Press, 2001.
- Medicine Bag: Usually a small pouch, worn by some Indigenous people, that contains sacred items, symbolizes personal well-being and tribal identity.
- Four sacred healing plants: *Asemaa*-Tobacco-East direction, offering prayers to the Creator, where Grandfather sun rises every morning; *Giizhik*-Cedar-South direction-a purifier, a cleansing; *Mashkodewashk-Sage*-West direction, a purifier, the setting Sun; *Wikingash*-Sweetgrass-North direction, purifier; braided, signifies the hair of *Ashkaakamigokwe* (Mother Earth), each three sections meaning mind, body, and spirit.
- Eagles are honored: Ojibwe name *Migizi*–helper of the Creator; *Giniw*-(golden eagle) medicine bird.

- Eagle feathers are honored: Ojibwe names *Migizi miigwan*-bald eagle feather; *giniw miigwan*-golden eagle feather; *miigwanan* -feathers (plural form).
- Great White Father in Washington D.C.: President Andrew Jackson. During his political rise, he distinguished himself with his ability to exact ruthless military victories over indigenous people. His legacy is forever "Indian removal" from lands to make way for white settlers. Source: *Wondery American History Tellers*, https://wondery.com/shows/american-history-tellers/, 4/18/18.
- *Eya'* : Ojibwe; English, Yes
- *Asemaa:* Tobacco; *Manoomin:* wild rice
- Ojibwe Clan people: There are 21 Ojibwe clans, each symbolizing an animal, fish, or bird species.
- Ojibwe bands: Each band is self-governing headed by an elected council and hereditary chiefs.
- *Miigwech:* Thank You
- *Gigawaabamin*: See you later.
- Half-breed Tribal Police: Peace officers hired by those Native American tribes which have a constitutional government on reservation, as opposed to hereditary chiefs.
- Chief James Doolittle: Chief *Wegimawebitang*, recognized as one of the hereditary Bad River chiefs after *Kish-ke-ta-wug's* death in 1888 at age 85 in Odanah, Wisconsin.
- Consumption: White plague, tuberculosis, or T.B.
- Tribal allotment land or *Dawes Act of 1887*: Giving the federal government the right to remove Indians from their land and place them on remote reservations, and divide allotted members 80 acres in parcels, the remaining sold, given to white settlers, ranchers, timber and mining companies. The government policy was: the tribe would dissolve and the reservation would disappear. Secretary of Interior leased Indian land to non-Indians,

controlled tribal funds, and determined when to pay money to tribal members.

- *Pow-wow*: Native dance, a gathering to celebrate life.
- Swamp tea: Labrador roots, Ojibwe pick and gather leaves in spring to autumn, boiling the leaves for beverage and medicine, sweetening with maple sugar.
- Grandfather: Chief *Kish-kish-ke-ta-wug*: Leader of the Chippewa Tribe, at Bad River Chief, signer of 1854 Treaty, born 1770, died 1888. Source: Article by Mike Munnell in *News from the Sloughs Historical Sketch*,1996.

Chapter 2

- Indin: Indian, some Ojibwe speakers with a "rez accent" say "Indin" or "Injian" (usually Indin).
- Indian Boarding Schools:

  Key dates in American Indian Education:

  1794: United States signs first Indian treaty for Indian Education. A formal agreement between two or more nations, when the government law was touched by the feather pen.

  1860: First Indian Boarding School: Captain Richard Pratt founded Carlisle Indian Industrial School, Pennsylvania. "Kill the Indian in him, and save the man" by removing children from reservations and family and to civilized ways through education. The effect was cultural genocide. Boarding schools operated this way for nearly another century. Native children from 140 tribes attended Carlisle, however only 158 students graduated. The largest number of students were Lakota, Ojibwe, Seneca, Oneida, Cherokee, Apache, Cheyenne, and Alaska Native. Over 10,000 plus students attended Carlisle.

  1928: A report to Congress: Indian boarding schools failed to provide skills relevant to Indian youths. Abuse, kidnapping, malnutrition, and death continue for another 40 years.

1968: Navajo Nation established first tribally-controlled college.

1972: Federal Indian Education Act within the U.S. Dept. of Education.

1989: American Indian College scholarships.

2001: Sovereign Nations Scholarship Fund Endowment.

Source: American Indian College Fund.

- Boarding School Experience: As early as 1856, Ojibwe children were taken from their families and reservations and placed in government, Catholic, or other Christian denomination Indian Boarding Schools, where school officials beat them if they spoke their Native/Mother tongue or practiced the traditional ways and customs.
- Elder: An older person respected by the community.
- Four Directions: Smoking a Peace Pipe: Cedar-South, acts as a purifier: Sage-West, a purifier: Tobacco-East, offering prayers to the Creator, giving thanks: Sweetgrass-North, a purifier; braided, signifies the hair of Mother Earth with each braid meaning mind, spirit, and body.
- Smoking a pipe: A tube with a small bowl at one end used to smoke tobacco, a way to communicate with the Creator.
- Long house: A formidable barrier that encircled the entire village. Build with saplings bent forward, making a hoop. Leaving doorways at each end.
- Louise Starr: Minnesota Chippewa Tribe, Fond du Lac enrolled member, Sawyer village, second wife to Frank Dooliittle.
- Warden Morgan: The official in charge U.S. Federal Leavenworth Prison.
- Grip: A traveling bag, a satchel or a cloth container, luggage.
- Paddy wagon: Patrol wagon with bars.

Chapter 3

- Three sister plants: Corn, beans, squash.

Chapter 4

- Samuel Campbell: White Indian Agent: Conspiring with the Stearns Company to cheat tribal members. A federal audit led to Campbell's dismissal, revealing he "stole" $30,000 of Indian timber money. Source: Patty Loew, *Indian Nations of Wisconsin*, Wisconsin Historical Society Press, 2001.
- Indian Ceremony Marriage: Arranged by parents or guardians with little formal ceremony.
- Fond du Lac Reservation: The Fond du Lac Band is one of six Chippewa Indian Bands that makes up the Minnesota Chippewa Tribe. The reservation was established by the La Pointe Treaty of 1854. The reservation is *Nagaajiwanaang* which means "where the water stops."
- Treaty of 1854: President Millard Fillmore and the Ojibwe created four reservations: Bad River, La Courte Oreilles, Lac du Flambeau, Red Cliff to hunt, fish, and gather in the land they had ceded. The government then opened up Ojibwe land to non-Indians in Wisconsin.
  Source: Wisconsin History/Native American Studies, 2001.
- Stearns Company Store: A non-Indian business on the Bad River Reservation. Owned three sawmills, blacksmith shop, icehouse, barbershop, miles of railroad tracks, and the "company store." The company cheated tribal members, arranging timber contracts that were three times lower than fair market value.
  Source: Patty Loew, *Indian Nations of Wisconsin*, Wisconsin Historical Society Press, 2001.
- U.S. Bureau of Indian Affairs: Was formed on March 11, 1924, by Secretary of War, John Calhoun, who created the agency as a division within his department, without authorization from the United States Congress. He appointed McKinney as the first head of the office which went by several names, to oversee and

carry out the Federal Government Trade and Treaty relations with the tribe. Source: https://en.wikipedia.org/wiki/Bureau_of_Indian_Affairs

Chapter 5

- Sons of Frank and Mary Houle-Doolittle: Joseph and Frederick Doolittle: Bad River Enrolled.
- First wife: Mary Houle-Doolittle-Laundry, Minnesota Chippewa Tribe, Fond du Lac enrolled, Indian Ceremony marriage.

Chapter 6

- Black Robes: The Jesuit Missionaries: Priests, Nuns sent to convert the Ojibwe to Christianity and divide the Native people. Source: Patty Loew, *Indian Nations of Wisconsin*, Wisconsin Historical Society Press, 2001.
- Ojibwe Bad Spirit: *Maaji-manidoo.*
- *Mindimooyenh:* Old woman (a term of respect)*; Mindimooyag* Old women (plural form – term of respect).
- Small Pox Blanket: Natives were vulnerable to European contagious diseases. Natives believe the smallpox was in the army wool blankets.
  Source: John Koster, "Winter Rabbit," *Wild West Magazine*, 2017.
- Woodlands: Ojibwe People whose homeland are located near lakes and rivers of northern forests/descendents of *Algonquian* group.
- Sister School Little Church/School: Ojibwe Natives' name for the *Franciscan Sisters of Perpetual Adoration School* in Odanah.
- Mother Tongue: Native Language-Speech.

Chapter 7

- Many Nations: Federal Native tribes in the US (500 plus).

Chapter 8

- Carlisle Old Barracks: United States Indian Industrial School, Carlisle, Pennsylvania, from 1879 through 1918. Also known as the Carlisle Barracks, founded by Captain Richard Pratt.

- St. Patrick Catholic Church: Carlisle community from 1879 to 1918, practiced assimilation to transform more than 10,000 Native children from "savage" to Christian religion.
- Holy Communion: Is the third of seven sacraments received. It occurs only after receiving Baptism, and once the person has reached the age of reason (2nd grade) first confession (the first sacrament of penance) must precede the reception of the Eucharist (refers to Christ, Body (bread), Blood (wine). (Roman Catholic religion).

Chapter 9

- Carlisle Mounds of Dirt: A cemetery, a place where the federal government set out to destroy Indian ways of life and where children died in the process. Hundreds of native students were lost in a brutal turn-of-the-century experiment in forced assimilation. Article from: www.Philly.Com/News by Jeff Gammage, August 8, 2017.

Chapter 11

- George Curtis: Bad River Indian, convicted of buying whiskey on the reservation; *Duluth News Tribune*, 1917.
- Sugar Bush/Camp: Ojibwe tap maple trees, collecting the sap into buckets of birch bark, boiling the liquid over hickory-bark fire until it turns to sugar, or is mixed with food or stored.
- United States Citizenship Act in 1924: President Calvin Coolidge and Congress passed and granted Citizenship to all Natives born within the United States on June 2, 1924. Natives have long struggled to retain their culture. Until 1924, Natives were not citizens of the United States. Yet after the Indian Citizenship act was passed, some Natives were not allowed to vote because the right to vote was governed by states. Until 1957, some states barred Natives from voting. Source: National Archives, General Records of the U.S. Government.

Chapter 12

- Christian/Catholic Church: An Indian was to be taught authority, love of labor, industry for employment, to make a civilized man of him. Without these elements, he will be lazy, shiftless, feeble-minded. Source: Patty Loew, *Indian Nations of Wisconsin*, Wisconsin Historical Society Press, 2001.
- Blue Coats: U.S. War Cavalry.
- Blood Memories: Cultural genocide at Indian boarding schools. Destruction of native culture, language, spirituality of American Indian children, death of thousands of students through disease, hunger, malnutrition, trauma, and grieving across Indian country. Blood Memoires/historical trauma. Source: Tom Weber/Host *MPR News,* 2016.

Chapter 13

- Conscientious Objectors: Torture technique known as "high cuffing." Wikpedia: Selective Service Act 1917; Duane Stoltzfus, *Pacifists in Chains: The Persecution of Hutterites during the Great War*, Johns Hopkins University Press, 2014.
- Chief *Osagie*: Ojibwe, Fond du Lac Chief, Wisconsin Point head man, a signer of the 1854 Treaty. In 1915, the Unites States Steel Company began digging up *Osagie* ancestors' graves. In 1916, a vision came to him. "Their bones must not be disturbed. This nation will see a terrible fire, a plague, and the bloodiest war!" Source: Donna Ennis, "The Heavens Became Black; The Curse of Wisconsin Point," *Indian Country Today*, October 25, 2014.

A vision – he could see our future

Illustrations

Acknowledgments

There are Natives and non-Natives who gave me the skills, knowledge, confidence, and inspired me to write Grandfather's story.

Arrowhead Regional Arts Council awarded the writing grant to complete the book. Ashley Kolka–ARAC, General Manager, coached me one on one with the on-line grant application.

Adult Leaning Center Staff–John Herold, support, guidance, encouraged me to keep writing. Gina Temple-Rhodes, technical advice, finding documents, researching, editing, encouraged me to apply for ARAC grant. Kristine Rikkola, Marilyn Myry, motivated and nominated me for interview in *The Women Today* magazine. Barb Durst, first instructor, patience, pep talks, encouraged me to join writers' group. Jean French, student, listening, reading my stories.

Family–brother Fred, storytelling, reading, suggestions, trying to identify boarding school photos. His kids–Jerry, Lori, Darcy–teaching me computer skills.

Friends–Tom and Rose Holten, Gene and Barb Redlich, John and Arleen (Fairbanks) Heyd, Mary Picard–listeners, supporters through the years.

Fond du Lac Historical Society–Carol Jaakola, Ella Couture Netand, Christine Carlson, Louwanna Johnson–researching, Carlisle school records, newspaper articles, copying.

Mike Munnel–Spiritual Elder, research and obtaining Bad River Chief *Kish-ke-ta-Wag* stories.

Donna Schilling's Writers' Group–sharing, trusting, patient, never judging, urging me to write grandfather story. Cornelia Dacey and Coral McDonnel–computer gift–Donna Churchill, Sue Crawford, Kerry Everett, Pat Joyelle, Mary Ann Koeller, Bonnie Malterer, Marlene Miller, Erin O'Daniel, Steve Sigford, Helen Kampa.

Writers' Square Table–Mara Hart-inspired me to write in the first person.

Marlene Wisuri–Publisher, researcher, graphic designer, friend, instrumental in getting grandfather book published.

Nancy Berg–ALC volunteer-editing, supportive, "boarding school children suffered."

Sandra Wright–friend, editing, encouraging, "this story has to be told."

Janis Fairbanks–reviewing the *Anishinaabemowin* words and orthography.

About the Author

Sharon Doolittle Shuck, an 80-year-old Ojibwe Elder from the Fond du Lac Reservation in northern Minnesota, began writing *Memories from the Tarpaper Shack*. After reading her grandfather's Leavenworth prison records; elders and writing groups inspired and encouraged her to write *Grandfather's Blood Memories and Unbroken Spirit*. This is her first book. She resides in Duluth Minnesota.

They come...

Brothers and Sisters from many Nations

They weep from hunger and thirst

They weep in sorrow and pain

They weep for a Mother's touch